"Parenting is never easy, but when a child is struggling with mental health issues, it is particularly difficult. This guidebook provides clarity and a path forward. A must-read for parents, loved ones, and anyone who may be struggling."

—**DR. LAURA BERMAN**, NY Times Best-Selling Author, Relationship Expert, TV, Radio, and Podcast Personality

"*The KrazyGirl (& Guy) Survival Guide* is not only a handbook filled with profound information and clinical advice but also a guide for those of us with a burning will to endure the storms of our own 'Krazyness.' Marci and Courtney share their stories and experiences with vulnerability and intellect, which urged me to open my heart, forgive myself, accept my Krazy, and learn to truly love and nurture my scared inner child, and finally set her free from the heartbreak which tied her to the past."

—**LINDSEY LAWLESS**, MEd

"Courageous, authentic, and insightful! The authors share their personal experiences of the trials and tribulations of being a family. Their three-prong approach of personal stories, expert opinions, and practical skills provide what is needed for moving through life's challenges with a steady hand. A how-to guide designed to move a family from fractured to functional, despair to hope, isolation to connection."

—**ERIC KISPERT**, LCSW, Relationship Expert

"The importance of wellness practices for physical and mental health is clear, and we are increasingly understanding the important role they play for physical and mental health. In this easy-to-understand guidebook, Marci and Courtney share their hard-earned knowledge, and pave a path forward for happier and healthier minds."

—**BERYL BENDER BIRCH**, Yoga Icon, Best-Selling Author of *Power Yoga*

"Marci Wolff Ober's entire life story has been leading up to this book. Her restless intuition has born her aloft over the detours of life wonderfully, carrying her to great wisdom and the insights she now inhabits. I have no doubt this book will help countless people who struggle with the challenges that life too frequently presents."

—**MARTYN BURKE**, Director, Producer, Screenwriter, and Author

"Relatable and easy to understand, while also a unique approach to mental health and wellness. For parents who need a clear understanding of how to support their child who is struggling, or individuals who struggle themselves, this comprehensive guidebook is incredibly helpful. As a clinical social worker, I recommend this book to all my clients!"

—**KALO MALONEY, LICSW**

"The high school chapter in the *KrazyGirl (& Guy) Parent Survival Guide* is perfect. I wish I had it to read when we started our journey through the mental health system. I think it should be in every pediatrician's, child psychiatrist's, psychologist's, and counselor's office and given to parents as required reading as soon as they seek treatment for their child. It is SO very well written and is filled with some of the most clear and concise information concerning all aspects of teen mental health I have ever read."

—**BONNIE PLANTE**, South Carolina, Warrior Mom

"If I had had this book when I was plunged into my daughter's mental health journey, the pages would have been dog eared and tear stained. I was scared, knew nothing, and had no experience. The knowledge provided by the variety of professionals and thoroughness of options provides guidance and hope. The voices of Marci and Courtney, their journey and triumphs, provide real-life examples of the struggles and triumphs that come with mental illness, and also provides needed hope and a clear path forward."

—**KIM WILSON**, Mother, Senior IT Project Manager

"As a practicing gastroenterologist, I see firsthand the mind-body connection and the havoc mental illness can wreak. This easy-to-read mental health manual contains so much valuable information, I not only appreciate it personally but am excited to recommend it to my patients!"

—DR. EDWARD BARBARITO, MD

"Marci and Courtney beautifully capture the good, the bad, the ugly of 'Krazy,' and the triumph of recovery in a book that is laced with humor amidst a background of pure raw emotion."

—JANIE SPEARS, JD, Recovered Anorexic

"I wish I had this comprehensive resource when my KrazyGirl was younger. I had to become a researcher, advocate, and an expert in school law, medications, and treatment options to get my daughter the help she desperately needed. It became a part-time job. The *KrazyGirl (& Guy) Parent Survival Guide* lays it all out for you in a clear, concise, and easy-to-navigate manner. I can also personally vouch for many of the experts cited as I had hired several of them to get my daughter to where she is today: a thriving college student."

—MELISSA GRIEGEL, Broadway Photographer/Reviewer, Parent of a KrazyGirl

"This guide is so relatable, and should be required reading for all of us. Because after all, who amongst us isn't, or doesn't know someone who is, at least a little bit Krazy! Thank you, Marci and Courtney, for this important work."

—SUSAN KLEIN, MA, Writer, Editor, and Warrior Mom

"This unique and valuable manual is an easy-to-understand compass and a road map forward—out of the darkness, toward sustainable mental health and wellness. I only wish I had this book when our family was in the thick of our challenges."

—BEV R., Atlanta, Georgia, Warrior Mom

"I have known Marci and Courtney personally and professionally for many years. Their exploration of both the subtleties and major themes of mental illness demystifies what is typically a murky and confusing topic. As a practicing psychiatrist working with children, teens, and adults, I believe this book is a must-have for parents, loved ones, and all who struggle with the challenges that mental illness brings."

—**BRUCE FRIEDMAN, MD**, Psychiatrist

"Talking authentically about mental illness is one of the most important steps to turning it into mental wellness. May the fresh air of truth that Marci and Courtney so bravely offer cascade into the hearts and minds of the many who stand broken, are close to breaking, and those who stand at their side] in support. The truth not only sets you free; it heals you and all you touch thereafter."

—**FIG ALLY**, Activist

"*The KrazyGirl (& Guy) Parent Survival Guide* is a brave and honest look at a family's struggle with mental illness. Both mother and daughter are very candid about their journey; this enables others to identify with them and ultimately learn from their experiences. A balance of insight and education, it's a vital aid to survival in the ever-changing waters of parenthood."

—**JARED CANTOR, RN**, ER Nurse

"As a mother and a psychologist, I have worked with many families in crisis, but when it is your own family, as I well know, all goes out the window. That is why this is such an important book for everyone to read. Which parent has never felt overwhelmed by the magnitude of raising a child? This is an important tool, filled with suggestions and instructions on how to careen through this perilous excursion. A definite must-read!"

—**DR. CARMELA SANSONE, PhD**, Practicing Clinical Psychologist

"Therapist Marci and her daughter, Courtney, have penned an honest and authentic account of their journeys to good mental health. Their outcomes and candor are inspiring! Look past the word 'krazy,' and you'll find a useful guide for parents and teens."

—**CAROL VAN DEN HENDE**, Award-Winning Author of
Goodbye, Orchid

"If parenting challenging, yet wonderful, children came with a universal manual, it would look just like this. This guide is nonjudgmental, relational, inclusive, practical, open to creative interpretation, and virtually indispensable for those of us familiar with this lifelong struggle. I wish it was available years ago."

—**SK**, a KrazyMama, raising KrazyGuys and proud of it!

"This book has so much information and so much heart. I saw things I went through, lessons I learned, and lessons I have yet to learn. It was a pleasure to read, and an honest joy to learn more about the complex topic of mental health!"

—**NAOMI K.**, Mom, IT Analyst

"I hope and pray you will never need this book, but the truth is, you or someone you know probably will. If you find yourself on the Krazy path of life, you don't want to travel without this masterful guide. A definitive, practical, and useful manual to help navigate the uncharted and unfamiliar world of Krazy, and come out stronger on the other side."

—**EDL,** Parent and Educational Consultant

"When Krazy happens in your life, you are fraught with panic, overwhelming concern, and hanging on for dear life, trying to hold it all together. You don't have the knowledge or experience to decipher your next step. What should I do? Who should I turn to? How can I get help ? This aptly titled 'survival guide' is an invaluable resource, providing much-needed help and guidance. It thoroughly explores a wide variety of treatments, provides professional resources, and offers much-needed support for those trying to survive. This book should be not only in everyone's library but also in their medicine cabinet, in case of emergency. Courtney and Marci's teachings, from decades of personal and professional experience, can help you and your loved ones not only survive Krazy but even come out a better person for doing so."

—**LDL**, Mother, Special Needs Educator

"This book normalizes and makes sense of issues that I believe everyone struggles with in their lives. Navigating the different types of mental health treatment options that are available can be overwhelming, as it is not a one-size-fits-all solution. Well, here you go! This is more than a book; it's genuinely a navigation and learning tool that also shows us that we're not alone!"

—**JAMIE SECOL, LCSW**, Therapist, Mother

"*The KrazyGirl (& Guy) Parent Survival Guide* is a necessary addition to any family with children, even if your children are not exhibiting any symptoms as described in this book. These brave authors (mother and daughter) unveil their own personal Krazy story as a baseline to the book. The transparency into their lives is mind blowing—only to find out it is the norm in society! Their message: 'Don't give up; there is help for you.' KG is also a path forward, a bible of sorts, offering up mental health education and a step-by-step guide to resources for recovery. Out with the 'one shoe fits all' and in with the 'what works for me.' Thank you, Marci and Courtney, for this inspirational gift to humanity!"

—**ROXY LOPEZ**, Artist, Musician, Journalist.

"The lesson in all of this is if you're not feeling well, something is wrong. It can be addressed, but you have to admit that something is wrong. Help is available. We must choose to dig deep and do the work. Living consciously is not easy. This amazing guidebook can point you in the right direction, and the authors bravely pave a clear path forward. Take it. You and your loved ones are worth it!"

—**SUSAN**, Federal Court Judge

"*The KrazyGirl (& Guy) Parent Survival Guide* is a truly unique and authentic self-help book that will provide hope, support, and relevant information for many families. Told from the perspective of both mother and daughter, it is truly inspiring and relatable while it helps guide anyone going through a mental health issue. Marci and Courtney's bravery in telling their stories allows the reader to feel safely guided by their recommendations and advice. Bravo to this genuine approach to helping others in the world of mental health. We need more Marcis and Courtneys in this world!"

—JENNIFER L. RODRIGUEZ, DLitt

"I love that the authors present both the parent and daughter's perspective. Their story is representative of what needs to be told: struggle, relapse, resilience, and a long-term approach are the truths about mental health that people really need to hear. The overview of the process is great, and the professionals who contribute do a good job of articulating their roles. Highly recommend this well-designed and easy-to-read guidebook."

—MK, Father, Substance Abuse Treatment Program Director

"As a parent and teacher, I found this book essential to understanding the impact mental health challenges have on both a parent and adolescent. The chapters in the book alternate between Marci's and Courtney's experience dealing with the Kraziness of adolescence. Understanding the perspective of both sides allows the opportunity to learn about mental illness on a deeper level. It's a book that will have a permanent place on my bookshelf, to reread and reference throughout parenting and teaching."

—BETH KIERNAN, Teacher, Mom

"*The KrazyGirl (& Guy) Survival Guide* helps people of all ages navigate the complexities of mental illness, personally and across their specific family dynamic. This book is filled with a plethora of top-notch, well-informed directions to take when mental illness is consuming you or a family member. It includes insight from top healthcare professionals and a map to help those struggling to move forward toward mental health and wellness. I highly recommend this book to anyone that is battling mental illness in any form themselves, or to help a loved one."

—NIKI CONDURSO, MFT, Mom

"I appreciate how the authors model vulnerability and openness in the worthy fight to end stigma around mental health. It is powerful to hear their firsthand accounts, woven in with meaningful professional opinions from across the treatment spectrum. Bravo, KGs!"

—MIKE GRANDE, Mental Health Advocate

"Coming from a family hugely impacted by mental illness, I found this book insightful, informative and truly eye opening. Admittedly, I'm not typically one to pick up a self-help book, but I've known Marci for about forty-five years (since our very own Krazy years!), so I was confident that this would be written from a place of pure love, honesty, and at least a touch of humor rather than filled with medical verbiage that for me always turns into a snoozefest. Mental illness is not pretty, but the depth, honesty, and willingness to bare their souls shared by Courtney and Marci as we walk with them through their journey is absolutely beautiful. The KrazyGirl motto, 'We're all a little Krazy; it's what we do with it that counts!' is absolutely brilliant and always puts a smile in my heart. And let's face it: it's true! *The KrazyGirl (& Guy) Parent Survival Guide* is definitely worth a first, second, and third read!"

—HELAINE SCOPE TEUSCHLER, KG

"This guide has come decades too late for many, just in time for some, and stands as a beacon for generations to come. The intuitive writing, authentic experiences, and high-quality contributions provide a full spectrum of lessons for the child, the parent, and practitioners. I don't think there is a more comprehensible guide that exists which provides a platform for growth and unity under the same topic as this one does."

—STEVEN DONOHUE, MSW, Guide, Father, Veteran, Entrepreneur

"This book is a must-read for any parent suffering through mental health challenges with their children. A true hands-on manual addressing strategies to help you and your child. Highly recommended!"

—**DONNA GALARZA, CN**, Functional Medical Nutritionist

"Chapter 7 Family Dynamics Roll Downhill will resonate with everyone, whether or not there is a history of mental health. I was intrigued by FABs (family attitudes and beliefs); it really should be a mantra for all of us. In fact I would be the president of the FABs fan club! With that said, I am also a believer of the learn, heal, and teach model. Once we can incorporate these topics, we as a society will make a difference in both our families' lives and the lives of others that we encounter."

—**DALE SCHULTZ LAZAROVITCH**, Nutritional/Health Coach (New Jersey)

"I wish I knew now what I did not know twenty years ago! I always talk about ADD/OCD as well as AC/DC, and this book and a little humor will surely go a long way to help so many people. If we talked about mental health like we talk about Covid, do you know how many lives might be saved??? Read this book! Talk about it with your friends. Let's bust the stigma!!"

—**DENISE CUOMO**

"As we surrender to travel down the road less taken, this fantastic guide book will connect you to a family of trailblazers who view life from both sides now, from up and down. Still, somehow, it's going to be your journey—not alone but with hope and promise."

—**BONNIE,** Long Island, NY

"Marci and Courtney are brave to be so resilient, humble, and willing to share their respective stories. I think it helps 'humanize' the imperfections of being (and raising) a teenager. I also loved how this book breaks down the different treatments for mental healthcare from the voices of those who are so respected in their fields. But most of all,

I wholeheartedly appreciate that this book doesn't necessarily seek to 'destigmatize' or 'normalize' mental health—because for those of us who have navigated these waters, we know there is nothing normal about being in 'KrazyLand.' Instead, their ability to legitimize the confusion and pain that's caused on this journey helps us to know that there's light at the end of the tunnel . . . as long as we continue to be resilient and lean in to the right resources who can help us find it."

—**KATE KENNEDY**, Domestic Badass

"A must-read for anyone, since we all struggle to some degree with mental health or know someone who does. Marci and Courtney take you on their very raw, intimate journey from rock bottom to thriving mental health maintenance. Their personal struggles and victories will give you hope that with love, knowledge, determination, and a lot of hard work, you can thrive again and 'be happy.' Their guide not only covers the challenges but also how to survive your triggers and make self-care a priority. We all deserve to find peace and happiness."

—**KATHY S.**, New Jersey

"A must have book for anyone trying to help a child, (or themselves), when suffering with mental illness. Courtney's courageous accounts of her time in KrazyLand during her adolescent years is sure to resonate with a young person feeling alone in their battle—and for a parent who feels helpless to take their pain away. Marci highlights the myriad of research, doctors, therapies, medications explored and lessons learned on Courtney's path to wellness. She expertly weaves and consolidates years of professional and personal experience into an easy to understand guide—a roadmap of sorts—for parents asking 'where do I start to help my child?' Before you google that question and travel down a never ending rabbit hole—read this book!"

—**RENEE**, Long Island NY

"Courtney and Marci's personal story of struggle and success provides an exceptional window into the very real world of the mental health treatment process. Mother, daughter and an impressive array of experts walk you through this process in a uplifting and informative way. A must read for families struggling to navigate the overwhelming world of mental health treatment."

—**MICHAEL MCKINNEY,** Executive Director at Pacific Quest. Father of 3 boys

The KrazyGirl (& Guy) Parent Survival Guide

by Marci Wolff Ober, LMFT
with Courtney Jessica Ober

ISBN 978-1-64663-592-4

Published by

 köehlerbooks™

3705 Shore Drive
Virginia Beach, VA 23455
800-435-4811
www.koehlerbooks.com

The
KrazyGirl (& Guy)
— *Parent* —
Survival Guide

Helping Your Child of Any Age
Thrive with Mental Health Challenges

Marci Wolff Ober, LMFT
with Courtney Jessica Ober

VIRGINIA BEACH
CAPE CHARLES

Table of Contents

Author's Note

*T*he *KrazyGirl (& Guy) Parent Survival Guide* is designed to help you in a variety of ways throughout your mental health journey. This is not an easy road to navigate, and we believe that nobody should have to travel alone.

The authors share their deeply personal stories in depth in part one, and also in each chapter, to provide context and meaning to the important clinical information presented in this manual. Part one also presents therapy and medication options, which are usually the basics of proper mental health treatment. Part two delves into additional elements to consider for long-term mental wellness. Part three is all about wisdom, strength, and hope. You may wish to share Courtney's words with a young person who struggles, as they will likely relate to her story and therefore be more open to the information she conveys.

Please take your time with this material. Read cover to cover if you like, or skip to a chapter or section of particular interest. We invite you to take what resonates with you as a jumping-off point, and leave the rest behind. Although we may use humor when discussing the entirely serious challenges of mental illness, we are also extremely sensitive to the painful struggles and incalculable costs that surely exist. We strive to present information that is easy to understand and also clinically sound, and apologize for any errors or omissions.

It is our sincere hope that this book will educate, enlighten, and support you as you travel forward. May divine guidance clear your path.

MWO

Introduction

I t was winter 2014 when my fourteen-year-old daughter, Courtney, ran away from home. After an angst-filled family vacation, she snapped and rushed from the house in the middle of a family movie night. Not one to do anything by halves, Courtney fled in the middle of a raging snowstorm, after dark, in her socks. Fortunately, her older sister chased her down and hauled her back home. When they returned, less than twenty minutes later, relief flooded my veins.

Despite the feeling in the pit of my stomach that things were not right, I remember how tempted I was to normalize this event by unpausing the movie and pretending nothing had happened. At the same time, the sad undertone of reality leveled me. I knew Courtney needed help. Her depression and anxiety were no longer "typical teen angst," and her symptoms weren't going to just go away. More than anything, as my two beloved daughters stood in the foyer with snow whipping in behind them and puddles forming at their feet, I saw the worry in Courtney's eyes and knew it mirrored my own. We feared the unknown. We were just landing in KrazyLand, and neither of us knew how long and winding this road would actually be.

Although I had essentially no personal experience of this journey at the time, it is a familiar one for many. The National Alliance on

Mental Illness reports that seventeen percent of US youth experience a mental disorder. That means that over eight million young people and the people who love them would likely empathize with the tableau that played out that night in my foyer. With such a large community, why did I feel so alone?

As a licensed marriage and family therapist, I had spent decades in mental healthcare. Yet even with all of my professional knowledge and experience, navigating the long and painful road out of KrazyLand as a mom was the most difficult and important challenge of my life.

My hope is that *The KrazyGirl (& Guy) Parent Survival Guide* will act as a meaningful compass for anyone who has felt the way we did that terrible night. This easy-to-understand guidebook is the elusive roadmap out of KrazyLand for any parent who has stayed up until sunrise, searching the internet for help about their child's severe mood swings, suicidal thoughts, or other concerning behaviors. Now on the other side of this long and painful journey, we are privileged to share everything we have learned to help anyone who struggles, whether personally affected or a loved one trying to help. Emotional freedom is not free, but it is available through knowledge and effort, and the results can exceed your wildest expectations.

Welcome to KrazyLand

"Toto, I have a feeling we're not in Kansas anymore."
—**Dorothy,** *The Wizard of Oz*

"Boy I want to warn you it'll turn into a Ballroom Blitz."
—**Sweet**

"*Where am I? What has happened to me? I thought I was just going about my life, living the dream. But something is not right. I am not myself. I'm missing things, not as sharp as I should be. I worry a lot, don't have much energy, and I feel exhausted all the time. In fact, I am not sleeping well, my mind races at night, and I can't get things out of my head. My relationships are not good either. My family and close friends say they are worried about me, but they seem more annoyed. Why should they be annoyed with me? They are the ones who are pissing* me *off! Something is just not right . . ."*

Can you relate? I certainly can.

I have a KrazyGirl. That's not surprising, because I *was* a KrazyGirl. I don't think I am anymore, but that may be debatable. I promise you: We'll address this question in the following chapters.

Maybe *you* are a KG? Or perhaps you love one? This book is your survival guide. You may ask, "What exactly *is* a KrazyGirl?" and "Why do I need a survival guide?"

A KrazyGirl, now called a KG, is a person (not necessarily female), of any age, race, class, or background, who is to some degree, freaking *out of their mind*. I don't mean your run-of-the-mill emotional human, but instead, one who is clearly on the KG spectrum. This spectrum ranges from moderately erratic moodiness and temperamental nature (Level One Krazy) to "What is going on here? Do we need professional help?" (Level Two Krazy), to "HOUSTON, we have a problem!" (Level Three, or Batshit Krazy). Please take no offense. We say this with great respect, and with all the love in our hearts. We are in this boat with you. Busting stigma with humor and connection is the KG philosophy and a very effective combination for wellness.

We are more than twice as likely to suffer from anxiety or depression in America than we are to drive a Chevy. Chew on that for a while. So, we need to get over any stigma that can be a hurdle to health. The plain truth is, "We're all a little Krazy. It's what we do with our Krazy that counts." This is the KG tagline. When we're informed and educated, we can move forward toward lasting mental health and wellness. This is what the KG movement is all about: moving from Krazy to KrazyEmpowered, both for ourselves and for the ones we love.

Levels of depression, anxiety, addiction, and suicide have reached epic proportions. We know this, and we see ads for medications all the time. But what exactly is mental illness? We may have some degree of understanding, especially if we're personally impacted. However, many people are still essentially in the dark when it comes to these matters. And sadly, stigma and misinformation are still very alive and well in America and around the world. Yet, according to the National Association of Mental Illness, one in five adults in the U.S. will suffer from at least one major episode of mental illness each year.[1] One in six

---

1   2019 or latest available statistics at the time of writing. Numbers cited will change from year to year.

young people ages six to seventeen will be diagnosed with a mental health disorder. More than *forty-eight million* people meet the criteria for an anxiety disorder. That's over nineteen percent of the population! Yet only forty-three percent of those diagnosed will seek treatment, even though anxiety is incredibly treatable. Even more tragically, the average delay between the onset of symptoms and beginning any treatment is eleven years! Suicide is the second leading cause of death in young people ages ten to thirty-four. There are actually *two hundred ninety-seven diagnoses* listed in the bible of mental disorders, the *Diagnostic and Statistical Manual of Mental Disorders* (DSM-5). Attention deficit disorder (ADD), obsessive-compulsive disorder (OCD), borderline personality disorder (BPD), WTF? (LOL!) These abbreviations can confuse—and actually minimize—the difficult reality that accompanies these life-altering conditions. We want to change this sad and avoidable reality and redefine the way we all look at mental health and wellness. This is the mission of the KrazyGirl Project, which is the name of our registered charity.

We refer to "KrazyLand" as the place where the "bad stuff" happens. The onset of symptoms, the wobble off center that life had previously rotated on—we wish to leave this place as far behind in the rearview mirror as possible. No one *wants* to go to KrazyLand, we get drafted in kicking and screaming. Why then, do so many of us find ourselves here? Is it *nature*—what we have inherited from our biological hardware or genetic soup (*I knew Uncle Bobby was trouble . . . do I need 23andMe now?*) Or is it *nurture*—our formative environments or learned software? It is probably some combination of both. This is one big reason why we need to open up our hearts and minds when we realize we have arrived in KrazyLand.

We all want to know the *why* of a situation, because that is part of our inquisitive human nature. Oftentimes, knowing why *is* important, because this knowledge can lead us to a better understanding of what to focus on when considering the menu of wellness options presented in the KGPSG. Knowledge *is* power, and more of the right stuff is certainly better. But early on in this journey, it is probably more important to focus on *what*. Meaning, what exactly is going on? What is causing these concerning behaviors? For teenagers and young people of all ages, the cause can be especially confusing! Hormones, friendship and relationship difficulties, school issues, moodiness, self-esteem concerns, eating or sleeping changes—they can all overlap, obscuring the root causes. This tangle can be extremely challenging to tease apart.

How then, can we begin to understand what all of this means? How do we deal with the significant challenges of mental health, if we, or our kid, or a loved one is suffering? That is what the KGPSG is all about, and is best approached with an open mind and a dash of humor. Please try to suspend any judgment or blame as you travel in this new land. Those blinders really get in the way and keep us stuck. KrazyLand is hard enough to navigate without complicating it more! So, are you ready for this ride? (*um . . . no . . . not really, can I please exchange my ticket? I will happily pay the cancellation and rebooking fee . . .*). Please don't worry, you are not alone! This guidebook will become your new best friend, and we are here for you every step of the way. Open up and see what can happen.

What follows in these pages is the plain truth about a wide range of topics about surviving and thriving with mental health issues. It is written with *love* from three different perspectives. The first viewpoint is my own: my early life as a Level Three KG, later as Courtney's mom while she traveled the long and hard road into and out of KrazyLand, and also from my professional vantage point as a practicing psychotherapist. It is difficult to separate who I am personally and professionally at this point in life; my entire worldview is shaped by all of these aspects. The second perspective comes from the deeply personal experiences of my beautiful daughter, Courtney, who is now a thriving, happy, healthy young adult. However, her path to wellness has not been an easy one. She shares in candid detail what it is like to suffer from mental illness as a teenager, in the spotlight of the #instaperfect world in which we currently live. The third vantage point comes from the many talented professionals who have generously shared their knowledge and expertise in these pages. Each expert we were fortunate enough to interview is widely respected, has many years of experience in their respective fields, and shares what it takes to be healthy and well in KrazyLand. We extend our deepest thanks to each.

This is not an easy club to be a member of, and nobody ever joins voluntarily. We cannot return our package of Krazy once we have received it. When it arrives on our doorstep like an unexpected box from Amazon, (*excuse me . . . this is NOT MINE! I did NOT order this. It must be the neighbors* . . .), it becomes ours to own and deal with. So, let's rise to the occasion. We can open this package with courage, and with curiosity if we chose to. What is inside can be difficult, confusing, emotional, and exhausting. However, if we approach this wisely, it can also contain many amazing possibilities. Our hearts will open up. We can become more connected with others. Our priorities will shift in unexpected ways, both large and small. None of us have asked to join this club, but we are members, nonetheless. You are one of us now. We love you already. Welcome to KrazyLand!

PART I

THE BASICS

CHAPTER 1

Marci's Story

"Baby, we were born to run."
—**Bruce Springsteen**

"I fight authority, authority always wins."
—**John Mellencamp**

"*O*K. Here we go, deep breath. It is OK to share your story; it is necessary. It gives context and credibility to what you are writing about. This is a survival guide for Krazy Girls, Guys and those who love them. Who was more Krazy than you were? Yes, sharing this is vulnerable, but that is what this whole book is about- taking risks, changing, growing, becoming less Krazy and more empowered. All of which takes a lot of courage. How can you encourage others to do this, if you aren't willing to take some risks yourself? Go ahead. Dive in . . . "*

I was born on Thanksgiving Day in 1961, to the song, "The Lion Sleeps Tonight." Yup. As my mother was birthing, *Wimoweh*. This fated event happened in a neighborhood of Brooklyn, New York; thus, I became forever known as "Marci from Canarsie." You can't make this stuff up. Only seventeen years old at the time, my mother was a teen mom. I never questioned these facts until I was fifty-seven,

and my oldest kid said very casually, "Mom, you were a *mistake*."
Tears sprung to my eyes.

"NO, I WASN'T!" I shot back at her. She didn't mean anything
bad by this statement, she just assumed it was obvious. What
seventeen-year-old would ever want to be a suddenly single mother?
Especially way back in 1961?

PsychoDad

I never knew my biological
father. My mom says they were
married when I was born and
they divorced soon after. I have
only one picture of him. He is
looking squarely at the camera,
holding a knife in his right fist,
one eyebrow queerly raised,
looking like a complete psycho.
My mom says he was holding that knife to cut a cake, but I have never
seen anyone holding a knife to cut a cake like that. So, I always thought
of him as my *PsychoDad,* at least fifty years before the term "psycho"
became popular.

My mother said he was mean. She pleaded with me not to go
looking for him, because she feared he may hurt us. This era was before
there was any internet, so I had no means to look for him until I was
much older. I spent many years of my young life fantasizing about who
he might be and hoping that he would someday come and take me away.
As an adult, I hired a private detective to try to find him. PsychoDad
was nowhere to be found. What I was able to locate, however, was his
lengthy police record, including numerous counts of *menacing. What
the hell is menacing*, I wondered. Maybe he really was a PsychoDad? I
guess my mom was right. She usually is . . . she's a member of Mensa.

From a very early age, I was Krazy. When I was four years old,
I was expelled from Ethical Culture Nursery school for cutting off
my sleeping neighbor's ponytail during naptime. I sort of remember
this. I was curious about what her pretty yellow hair would feel like

A young Marci from Canarsie

between those safety shears, which of course did not go over very well. (My sincerest apologies!) At six, I somehow managed to set the small stand of trees behind our row of brick houses on fire. Again, nothing bad was intended, it was just my hyperactive curiosity paired with an unfortunate outcome. I also have very clear memories of playing a game called "King of the Fire Hydrant" out in the street. The neighborhood kids would take turns clawing our way onto the fire hydrant in the middle of our block, and then hold on for dear life. Once atop the hydrant, we would proceed to get mobbed by all the other kids who were fighting for their turn on top. There was kicking, punching, and pushing, until we were ripped from our privileged perch and fell, bruised and bloodied, back into the street. It was a nasty game that makes Dodgeball seem like a weenie roast.

As I got older, my environment changed, but my emotional state did not. When I was six, my mom remarried. Jesse was a funny, loving, and fully invested husband and father. He even adopted me as his own child, giving me his last name. My parents went on to have two more kids. I always thought of them as my sisters. There was no stepfather. There were no half-sisters. They were all in. My parents loved me. However, for reasons I do not fully understand, I did not *feel* loved. I felt ugly. Fat. Alone. Confused. Miserable. And very, very angry. By age seven, I was prescribed Ritalin and started to see a child psychologist. Her name was Dr. Grossman, and she was really kind. When I went to see her, I would stare at a beautiful picture of a landscape she had hanging on her wall. She actually gave that painting to me when we moved to New Jersey when I was in third grade. What a sweetheart she was, and my first role model of a great therapist.

When we moved to New Jersey, I felt even more like a fish out of water. I tried my best to fit in, but I just could not get the lay of the new land, with all its grass, trees, and big houses and lawns separating them. I felt like an outsider, so I called upon my best Brooklyn street fighting techniques and attempted to teach them to the kids in my new suburban neighborhood. This strategy did not go over well, and I became the target of what felt like brutal, non-stop "teasing," (now called *bullying*). This only added gas to my raging internal fire. There was nowhere I felt safe, no place I belonged. By middle school, I started shoplifting, cutting school, and having severe emotional meltdowns. Eventually, I began to run away from home. At thirteen, I jumped out of my second-floor bedroom window to escape. My parents had installed a lock on the *outside* of my door to keep me in, but *I was not having that!* I kicked out my screen, jumped off the roof, hit the ground hard, and shattered my left leg. My poor parents and neighbors stood in stunned silence as the ambulance came and took me to the hospital. The very next day, I wrapped my thigh-high cast in a big green garbage bag, called a cab, and ran away again in the rain, this time on my crutches.

One bad choice led to another. I was designated incorrigible, made a ward of the state, and sent to a juvenile detention center. A month later, after my fourteenth birthday, I was transferred to the ancient state mental hospital at Overbrook. There was no such thing as a child or adolescent psychiatric unit back then. I was placed in the general population ward, which was a nightmare right out of a horror movie. I will never forget the mental hospital social dance, with people with actual frontal lobotomy scars asking me to dance. I broke out of there too, which is a funny story for another time. I now understand that I endured a lot of traumas along the way in these awful places, but no one was thinking about trauma back then. They were just trying to keep me in one place.

I was sent to The George Junior Republic (GJR). This was a reform school located in Freeville, New York. I always thought that was ironic, being locked up in Freeville. Of course, I ran away from there too, during a snowstorm, in my socks. I hitchhiked my way to a friend's house over two hundred miles away, sleeping in dumpsters and sharing meals with truckers along the way. I am so lucky that nothing disastrous happened to me during that time. I was apprehended a few weeks later and returned to the reform school. I was placed in the GJR jail, which involved isolation and harder labor.

That was a huge turning point for me, because I decided that I would play their game instead of running away again. I saw this as my exit strategy. My goal was to try my best to get out of there ASAP, whatever it took. The motto at the GJR was actually, "Nothing without labor." So, I worked my ass off and rose through the ranks of their student-run society. I earned my cigarettes in the token economy and over time achieved the coveted status of "mature citizen." I learned a lot over the 18 months I was there. I now credit my self-discipline and work ethic to that place. Although I did not know it at the time, what I really learned was some serious emotional regulation skills because in reality, all my other options at the time were much worse.

Slowly, my self-esteem began to rise through the efforts of my own hard work at the GJR. The pride I began to feel in myself was real. Feeling connected to my peers for the first time also helped. I learned how to direct my internal fire and energy, instead of letting it carry me away on the KrazyTrain. This was the first life-changing element of my personal transformation: *From Krazy to KrazyEmpowered*; my golden ticket. Whether a person internalizes or externalizes their pain, learning to intentionally direct emotional energy is the first and most necessary step to deal with Krazy. However, I must say, it has also taken me many other rounds of high-quality therapy at different points in my life to feel like a whole and complete person. Emotional freedom is certainly not free.

My road forward from that point was not easy, but it was much better than it had been previously. I came home from the GJR the summer before my senior year of high school. I did not attend school very much, nor did I continue to live at home for long. I moved in with a biker gang and they became my family. We partied way too much, that's for sure. My nickname was "JAP" (Jewish American Princess).

The Ant Hill Mob Motorcycle Club 1979, Marci lower 2nd from right

I was not offended, we all had nicknames. We laughed and cried together, we lived and loved. We were like any other KrazyFamily, in a wannabe Hell's Angels kind of way. This rag-tag group of outcast bikers gave me a leather jacket identity and with that, a feeling of safety. Members of the "Ant Hill Mob Motorcycle Club and the Ladies Auxiliary," would either take me to school on the back of a Harley Davidson, or I would hitchhike there. It was about twenty miles away. No surprise that I was absent for over ninety of the one hundred eighty days of school during my senior year, but they pushed me through anyway, and I graduated. Sadly, every one of our KrazyGuys died along the way, each in tragic ways. This includes my old boyfriend, John, who died in a drunk driving crash that he sadly caused. But all the KrazyGirls you see are alive and well, and a few are still some of my best friends to this very day, with one featured as an expert in the following chapters. Life can be very strange.

Although I faced many challenges in my younger life, I have always considered myself an extremely fortunate person. For example, when I graduated high school, Lady Luck, helped by my super smart mom, bestowed upon me a full scholarship to a good local state college, which is now is also Courtney's alma mater. College is where I found and fell in love with all things psychological. Finally, there were reasons on paper and proper names for the things I had experienced. Life was finally going my way! I loved the freedom and atmosphere of college life. I was head over heels for psychology and enrolled in every class and experience I could find in the department. I also began dating my husband during that time. However, I was still restless and craved adventure, so I invented a new and improved version of running away for myself.

After graduating college and working in the business world for a few years, I left New Jersey, this time sponsored by a company expense account, thanks to my job at Sanyo Business Systems. I moved to Los Angeles, where I lived in Hermosa Beach and rode my own Harley Davidson. I even took a solo bike trip up the California coast, camping along the way and riding my Harley across the Golden Gate Bridge! I earned my master's degree in Counseling Psychology from Pepperdine University, and then my first professional license while living in LA. I worked with homeless and runaway teens and got to do my sessions on the beach.

Marci and her Harley, 1987

Five years later, I received the opportunity to move to Anchorage, Alaska. There, I lived a lifestyle that was nothing short of a fairy tale. There were moose, glaciers, and a male to female ratio of ten to one, (the saying was, the odds are good, but the goods are odd!). I worked with Alaska Native families, started innovative programs at the psychiatric hospital where I worked, and traveled throughout that impossibly beautiful state doing community outreach. I extracted every bit of life I possibly could from those unique experiences before I finally got married and moved one last time, back home to my native New Jersey.

Marci in Alaska 1993

I established my psychotherapy private practice in the town I grew up in, had my two beautiful daughters, did yoga, and played Mah Jongg. I thought I was finally in the clear. My life was more than stable, so my KrazyDays must surely be behind me. Yeah, right. If only it were that easy. I know now that Krazy is a devious shapeshifter, that can take on many different forms.

Somehow, without my knowledge or consent, my family dynamics rolled downhill anyway, as they always seem to do. As much as I had consciously created the life I had always pictured, and told my kids *nothing* about my strange past, it all came back around and stuck to me like KrazyGlue. No amount of attachment parenting, homemade organic baby food, or the best private schools could prevent my beloved daughter from also becoming a KrazyGirl. Nature, nurture, or the stars, conspired to align in devastating ways, despite my best efforts. And that is where my individual story ends, and Courtney's begins. The dreaded torch was passed on.

These days, I reflect back on many things. I think about my father Jesse, who put so much love and kindness into me, and who sadly died so young. I think of my super-smart mother, who also comes with her own unique brand of Krazy. I feel badly that I put my family through so much pain back in those early years. However, I honestly believe that none of that could have been helped. My PsychoDad was a bonafide lunatic. I must have inherited some of his genetics, because I also have his strange tilted right eyebrow. Back then, there was not the degree of understanding about family dynamics or neurobiology that exists today. Thankfully, treatment options are worlds better now in every way possible. But none of that changes my early life experiences. Additionally, despite being born into a carefully cultivated life, and being the happiest little girl you could ever imagine, Courtney also succumbed to the Krazy.

I wish that none of us had to endure the suffering and devastation that we did. Experiencing that pain yourself or watching your kid struggle and being unable to alter their course is a horrible thing. Yet I would not trade any part of my life for any other life. I would not be who I am today if I did not travel my entire path. I am extremely grateful for all my experiences and blessings, and I love my life very much. Although, if I am being completely honest, during times of peak stress I still have the compelling fantasy of driving to Newark airport, swiping my Amex, and landing in Tahiti before anyone can even locate my car.

CHAPTER 2

Courtney's Story

"What a long, strange Trip it's been ... "
—Grateful Dead

"Girls become lovers, that turn into mothers,
so fathers be good to your daughters too."
—John Mayer

I f you are a teenager or young person reading this book, chances are we have many things in common. For starters, as I write this chapter, I'm twenty years old. I love music, animals, my dog, being with my friends, and spending time outdoors. I live on campus at my college and am a sister in a sorority. I sing all the time and perform in our campus a cappella group. At this point in life, I have learned what it takes for me to be happy and how to love myself. However, this has been a difficult process, and I have not always felt this way.

Looking back, I had a very happy childhood. I grew up in a small town in New Jersey, about thirty miles outside of New York City. My parents are married. I am the youngest of two children; my sister Jordan is two years older. She and I got along most of the time, and she was always there to support me. I had a lot of friends, did well in school, took dance classes, and played soccer; however, my true passion was singing. I performed in many places and was even

Happy little Courtney

Courtney as Dorothy in 4th grade

part of a touring rock-n-roll chorus, where I got to sing with some really cool people. Although I had a few bumps along the way, my childhood was great. How then, did a happy and healthy girl transform into the troubled teenager that I became? When did I become a KrazyGirl?

The signs started slowly. In middle school, I started to lose interest in activities that I had always enjoyed. I became awkward in social situations. I would refuse to go to events or would have a meltdown if my parents pushed me. Anxiety started creeping into my life and took the joy out of everything that I did. I questioned myself constantly, and eventually, I started to hate myself. That's when my cutting and eating issues began. I tried to hide all of this. I did not want to worry my parents or call any attention to myself. My situation went downhill fast. It soon became obvious to everyone around me that I was falling apart. I could no longer hide my pain.

I began therapy when I was in seventh grade. My therapist was kind, and speaking to her allowed me to open up about things that I was not able to understand. Time passed and my issues did not improve, so I went to see a psychiatrist who prescribed medication to treat my symptoms. The medicine did not help, and things began to snowball. In the fall of my ninth grade year I came down with mononucleosis, which made everything worse. My school life was slipping so I refused to attend class. I lost my friends, dropped out of activities, and became completely isolated. I began to fight with my parents. I could not sleep. I cried all the time. My self-hatred grew. By Halloween, I was in an extremely dark place.

I wore my emotions on my sleeve, dressing in all black and wearing huge amounts of makeup. Self-harming was an everyday activity, and my parents were frantic. Even though my mother was a therapist, she couldn't help me. None of the solutions we had tried were successful. As my depression and anxiety got worse, suicidal thoughts crept in. I wanted to die. I slept in bed with my mom because taking my life during the night had become a real possibility. My racing mind was completely out of control. I was hospitalized three times during my ninth grade year for my own safety. In addition to thoughts of suicide, I also began to have auditory and visual hallucinations.

This period of my life was so confusing and horrible. Each time I had to go to the hospital it was terrible. Every time I returned to school it was humiliating. I did not know what to say, and people started avoiding me. I was a zombie in class, and I could not shake the feeling that everyone was staring at me or laughing behind my back. I honestly do not know how

Dark days

I survived it all. Even writing about this now makes me very sad.

I barely got through that year, even though it seemed like we had tried everything possible to help me. My parents decided to take a radical step. My mom found a program located in Hawaii, so the summer before my tenth grade year I began my journey at Pacific Quest. PQ is a wilderness therapy program built around an organic garden, tucked far up in the hills on the Big Island. I did not want to go and was a wreck when I got there, weighing less than a hundred pounds. The whole thing was a shock to me. We lived on the land and grew all the food we ate. This was really hard work. Therapy was all day, all the time: in the garden, at the volcano, or on the beach. It wasn't just talk therapy, but also included many other challenges and Hawaiian rituals that made me see myself and life in different ways. I did a three-day solo in the sugarcane fields, with only bamboo sticks and a tarp to create my shelter. This program helped me become more self-reliant and taught me to treat myself with healthier self-care habits. I also learned to connect with other teens again, a skill that I had struggled with since my mental health had spiraled out of control in middle school. It was a wonderful experience and I left PQ full of hope.

After coming home, I returned to school with a new and healthier mindset. With my newly acquired skills, I was very optimistic. I did not understand it at the time, but my school environment was actually causing me to feel worse. The preppy, elite nature of the private school I had been in since sixth grade had caused me to judge myself in a harsh way. This hypercriticism gave way to a constant

Pacific Quest

comparison of myself to others, most of whom were extremely different than I was. I tried to fit in at the expense of my mental and physical health, but I began relapsing again. It seemed as though everything I had learned in Hawaii just slipped away. After another hospitalization for a suicide attempt, I switched schools and got a new therapist. Big change was necessary.

Beginning my eleventh grade year in public school was not an easy thing to do. Fortunately, this school had many support systems available to me. I was able to enroll in a program specifically for kids with mental health issues. My class had just four students. Rather than changing classes, the teachers would come directly to our classroom. The workload was easier than it was at my private school, but at that point I was in no position to challenge myself with rigorous academics. Even the thought of being in a regular classroom of thirty kids was overwhelming for me. Slowly, I regained my ability to learn and socialize. By the end of my eleventh grade year, I moved into regular classrooms. I even took AP classes and did some dual enrollment classes at community college. As I improved at school, I also continued to work on my mental and emotional health. I participated in a therapy group with my parents. This taught us skills necessary to regulate emotions. As time passed, I became more successful in other areas of my life, participating in things like the National Honor Society and Yearbook Club. I even had the privilege of singing the national anthem at my graduation! By the time I completed high school, I was a regular, college-bound teenager. I was accepted into my dream college early decision, and the future looked bright. We had a big graduation party at my house, and everybody breathed a deep sigh of relief.

Courtney Graduates High School!

Unfortunately, the summer before starting college, my anxiety returned. I could not imagine the idea of being away from home. I began to play out scenarios in my mind, and of course, none of them were good. I worked at a summer camp and spent a ton of time with my boyfriend, but even with all of those distractions, I could not shake the concern I felt about going away to school. I arrived at college a week early to participate in a music camp. My parents helped me move into my dorm room. After my belongings were hauled up and we had lunch together in the dining hall, we said our tearful goodbyes. They went home and I was all alone at school. Even though as a kid I went to sleep away camp and on a cross country tour with my chorus, at this point I was scared to death to be alone. Luckily, one of my friends from private school was moving in a few days later. I constantly reminded myself of this fact and prayed that being with him would help my anxiety fade away. When he finally arrived, I clung to him like a life raft. He was so kind to me, and we spent all our free time together. Honestly, he is the reason that I did not end my life in my dorm room a few months later. Was it not for him, I would not be writing this book and sharing my journey with you today. Thank you from the bottom of my heart, George!

As the semester progressed and my classes became more demanding, I began to feel those old feelings of depression build up again, just like in my early years of high school. This time, I was alone with these emotions despite all my years of therapy. I tried carrying on, ignoring them, and I even talked to a counselor at school in addition to my therapist and doctor. My situation did not improve. I will never forget my eighteenth birthday when my parents came up to school. They were smiling and handing me presents but were stopped by an outburst of tears and my admission that I was feeling depressed again. We talked to the school and my home counselor, and we all agreed that I would try to push through, using my therapy skills and leaning on the support team I had in place at school. This method did not work. By the time Halloween rolled around, I was dreading everything in life. Every night before I went to bed, I prayed I would not wake up the next morning. I had to leave my classes because of panic attacks. I quit my a capella group and spent my time with George or alone in my dorm room. There came a point when I could no longer handle my depression. After more than two years of being clean, I relapsed and self-harmed. I told my parents that I was not safe being away at college anymore. I took a medical withdrawal and we packed up my room in sad silence.

Leaving was so hard for me. On the one hand, I was relieved to go, but on the other hand, I could not believe that things had come to this again. This was my rock bottom. I was eighteen years old, and I was back down to a hundred pounds, a shell of a person. *I knew I had to fight for my life, or I would lose it this time.* I made the decision to stand up and fight for myself. Although I had been a vegetarian, I chose to eat meat again. I went into another outpatient treatment program, but this time as an adult. I looked at the others in this program of all ages and with all kinds of issues. I made the decision at that point that I would not be fifty years old and still fighting my terrible depression and anxiety. This was my turning point. I became willing to do anything I needed to do to get better and stay better. I gave it all I had this time and dove really deep into myself. I finally faced past trauma I had never dealt with before. I followed all treatment recommendations to the letter, and slowly I began to get better. I owned responsibility for my recovery and was determined to never go backwards! I transferred to a college closer to home, commuted for a semester and then felt ready to move onto campus.

Today I am happier and healthier than I have ever been, and I can honestly say that I love my life. Not that everything is perfect all the time, but I don't let small issues or setbacks get in the way of my happiness or affect the way I feel about myself anymore. I try to handle challenges with courage and a positive mindset. I am taking more risks and they are paying off. I joined a sorority and am now the wellness chair. I teach my sisters yoga and self-care techniques. I was accepted into the campus a cappella group, and I just got my first solo. I love my school, my social work major, my classes, and my friends. I continue to practice self-care habits that keep me healthy and strong. My mental health is my number one priority because I am never going backwards. I have learned these lessons the hard way. This new chapter in my life has now become my reality. I am grateful every single day for this, and I will never take it for granted.

Courtney
Soprano

KrazyGirls & Guys, I write this book for you. You are not alone. You may not have gone through all that I have, or you may be going through more. Our roads are all different, but our feelings are the same. We are sensitive people and life is not always easy for us. If you are struggling, *please have hope!* It takes work to be well, but it is well worth the work. Open up your mind and your heart and fight hard for yourself. Do not give in to anybody else's truth but your own. Be you and march to your own tune in life, but also accept help and use it to your best advantage. This may sound strange, but I would not trade all that I have been through for anything, because it has made me who I am today. You also can feel this way, I promise! Please love yourself. Believe in yourself. Be brave. I am here for you, and I can't wait to hear how your journey progresses.

CHAPTER 3

Therapy: Help Is on the Way

"Give me therapy, I'm a walking travesty,
But I'm smiling at everything."
—All Time Low

"I can see clearly now; the rain has gone.
I can see all obstacles in my way . . . "
—Jimmy Cliff

MARCI

What a wonderful opportunity for a practicing therapist and lifelong lover of therapy to have the pleasure to delve into this subject! Why am I *so into* therapy? I guess this question is essentially at the very heart of who I am. I truly and completely believe in the concept of "human psychological evolution." I use this term to refer to the possibility that we, as individuals and as a species, can *grow*. We can become *more*. We have the opportunity to evolve into better people. How does this evolution happen? Usually, it comes about as a result of going through our most painful life experiences. We all go through hard times. We can become "broken open" when these things occur, or we can become closed down and bitter. We can choose to hold a mirror to ourselves to improve, or we can shy away from the challenge and shrink. The choice is ours alone to make, but this choice will direct the path our lives will ultimately unfold upon.

Chinese symbol for crisis/
opportunity

One reason for my love of therapy is that if we choose to grow at our critical junctures, receiving some professional guidance can make a tremendous difference in how we manage these crossroads. We all have what I refer to as *opportunities in the crisis*. In fact, the Chinese symbol for crisis closely resembles the symbol for opportunity! The sooner we embrace this potential, the more things can improve in our lives.

It appears that KGs are particularly sensitive to something I refer to as "Messages from the Universe." At this point in my life, I try to pay careful attention to these messages when they first appear. The longer I ignore messages, the stronger they seem to tap upon my head. I prefer a light tap to a baseball bat upside my skull these days, so I really try to stay open. In fact, I have come to rely on this phenomenon for direction. The instinct to move towards or away from people or situations usually proves to be remarkably in our best interests. The quieter my Krazy is, the more I can listen for and receive this important source of personal guidance.

Fortunately, many wonderful therapists along the way have assisted me on my evolutionary journey, and I can't imagine that Courtney would be where she is today without good therapy. As a therapist myself, I try my best to meaningfully engage with every single person that I work with. Therapy is very personal to me, with great significance. These are some of the reasons why I love therapy. Remember in the opening chapters when I said that no one wants to be a member of the KrazyClub? I can't think of one person who ever voluntarily signed up. However, when you find yourself in KrazyLand, and really need things to get better, you will need to dig down deep into what is going on in your life. You must figure out what has led you, or your loved one, to the tipping point of Krazy. These are not easy questions and figuring out the answers is not straightforward. Hard times call for powerful measures.

Who are the folks that can best guide us through our most painful and confusing times, besides well-meaning friends and family? (Ghostbusters . . . ?) A good therapist! These special people are light workers in this world. Frequently, those drawn to this profession have gone through a lot themselves, truly desire to help others, and have a growth mindset that evolves and changes over time. Early on in my career, I thought I was a pretty good therapist. I had gone through my Batshit Level Three KrazyDays and learned a lot. My practice thrived, so I must have been doing something right. But after my long and winding road-trip with Courtney, I *know* I became a better therapist, and a better human being. My level of "got to pay your dues if you want to sing the blues, and you know it just ain't easy" understanding of life changed for the better through those terrible times. (Unless I am in rush hour traffic. Then I still need a lot of work!) The insight and compassion we can experience through pain and growth is the light side of the darkness. The Yin and the Yang. The human potential to reflect, grow, feel, and heal. We do the work for ourselves, for our loved ones, and for the future generations that will come behind us, as they ultimately must deal with the baggage we leave behind. This is why I am a Therapy Fangirl. Always and forever.

COURTNEY

Imagine being distressed, depressed, or overwhelmed to no end and feeling like you have nobody to confide in or talk to. So many people face this difficulty and would be so much better off if they were in therapy. Having a therapist by my side, through the good and the bad times, has been essential for my mental wellbeing. I honestly do not know where I would be if it was not for my amazing therapist. She has helped me through the good, the bad, and the ugly. Without having someone to talk to, things tend to get bottled up, confused, and built up. This suppression is terrible for your mental health.

My experience with therapy began when I was twelve years old. I went to a play therapist to help me with my self-esteem and social anxiety. In my weekly meetings with Joyce, we talked a lot about the problems that I was facing in school. She helped me work through my issues with the "mean girls" who were bullying me and causing me to feel bad about myself. We used toys and art materials to get my negative feelings out of my brain and onto the table. Once on the table, we would work with them. Beginning therapy when I was younger was good for me, and I continue this practice today.

After I outgrew play therapy, I started seeing my current, awesome psychologist, Laura. Not only could I talk with her about what was going on in my life, she also taught me skills that have helped me in so many ways. Starting therapy with someone new was scary. Every time I rehashed my painful life experiences, it made me sad and insecure *at that moment*. However, to help me, she needed to get to know my background, the things that helped me and the things that had hurt me. I had to go deep into my life situations and look at the way my brain works so that I could better my mental health. My sessions with Laura have been so helpful. I really benefit from talking through what is happening in my life with her. I have also learned to understand things from a different viewpoint. When I am not feeling well, I tend to be dark and cynical, but Laura helps me put things into a better perspective in my mind. Attending group therapy for skill-building also helped me learn and practice new ways of coping with my anxiety and depression. These skills have helped me deal with my challenges in much better ways. I use these skills daily, and I also teach them to my friends to use when they are going through hard times.

When I think about the benefits of therapy, the first thing that comes to mind is that it is necessary for people who are struggling with mental illness or difficult challenges. However, therapy is not just good for people who suffer from mental illness. I believe that everyone can benefit from therapy. It provides an outlet to talk about your feelings and what is going on in life. Yes, you can talk about these things with parents, friends, teachers, or other people. But having a therapist means that you can express *everything* that is going on inside you with somebody who is not going to judge you or tell anybody else. When I need to ask questions, rant, cry, scream, or celebrate, my therapist is always there for me.

It is also important to understand what it takes to succeed in therapy. For starters, having an open mind and being completely honest with your therapist are both vital parts of making therapy work. Additionally, being truthful and honest *with yourself is* extremely important. If you are lying to yourself, or to your therapist, you will not progress. Having an open mind with any information that is given to you is also essential. If you just sit there and "OK" your therapist, never absorb any new information, or fail to put their advice into practice, therapy will not help. Yes, this definitely takes courage. This is why therapy is really for the strong not the weak, as some people may think.

Finding the right therapist really matters, because you need to feel like you connect with them in order to talk openly and feel comfortable. It also helps to choose a therapist who is skilled in the areas that you need to work on. For example, if you have a background of trauma, you will not want to go to a therapist who has never dealt with that issue before. Instead, you would want to go to someone who is specially trained in EMDR (eye movement desensitization & reprocessing), Cognitive Behavioral Therapy (CBT), or another type of trauma-based therapy. Therapists specialize in areas where they have skills. Ask people you trust for referrals. People who have gone through hard things love to share what has helped them if they are asked. Therapy can make all the difference between moving forward in your life or staying stuck in the same old patterns.

I am sure it is no surprise that I plan to be a therapist. I am currently studying social work in college and love every minute of it. I am also minoring in something called contemplative studies, which is yoga, meditation, and other paths toward wellness. I am the Wellness Chair of my sorority and get to lead events such as face mask or yoga socials. I love the feeling I get when I help someone. I want to be a child therapist in particular, because I enjoy working with kids and helping them grow and change. I try my best to have a positive impact on people's lives. As I have shared, therapy is so important to me. I sincerely hope that you will take this information and use it to better yourself. Therapy can be amazing if you are open-minded, courageous, and honest. It can change your life if you allow it to.

Creating a positive and productive therapy experience involves planning!

Let's get to the meat and potatoes (or tofu and veggies) part of this chapter. What is therapy? What types of therapy and therapists exist? What sort of help will be the most helpful for me, or my loved one? How do we access this? What are the Levels of Care? How can I tell if a therapist is a good fit for me or not? These questions can be really confusing, especially if we are going through a mental health crisis. So, let's dive in. Therapy 101, here we come. (*Must we? I was planning on watching* Dancing with the Stars, *but, ok, I guess . . .*)

Consider the following elements of therapy as you choose your best path forward. The more research you can do in advance, the better your experience will likely be. Like a good hair day, this doesn't just happen, it takes effort and planning. But you got this! #KrazyEmpowered

- Determine as specifically as possible what you are seeking therapy for. What issue(s) are you or KG facing? For example, depression, substance abuse, grief, family problems?
- Research the best licensed professionals in your area.
- Find providers that specialize in the area you are seeking help for.
- Understand specialty approaches to therapy and consider expert advice (EA).
- Make sure the therapist's personality, or fit, is a good one for you.
- Consider the appropriate level of care. Scale up or down as necessary over time.
- Understand insurance and financial aspects and be wise about these choices.
- Be willing to be honest, dig deep, and work hard. Go all in. Own it, embrace it, work that updo. You got this!

Determine as specifically as possible what you are seeking therapy for. What issue(s) are you or KG facing?

In the beginning, when things are just beginning to go Krazy, you might not understand exactly what is happening. The symptoms that you or your loved one are experiencing may be confusing. Admitting that something is not right and choosing to do something about it is a big first step forward. Identifying the problems that are present and trying to put a name to them, *(i.e., depression, anxiety, addiction, food issues, school-related, relationship problems,* etc.) is important to obtain the proper assistance. As you will see shortly, the best therapy outcome comes from matching the issue with the proper treatment. It is common for people first entering therapy to have some resistance or mixed feelings about getting help. If you are new to therapy, congratulations on being willing to get the help you need and deserve! Things are about to get much better.

Research the best licensed professionals in your area.

There are many types of therapists that practice counseling and psychotherapy. When considering therapists, ensure that the provider you are considering has an active professional license in the state where they practice. This requires that the therapist has had a minimum level of training and verification to achieve their professional license. This may be as a psychologist (a doctoral degree of licensure, who may also conduct psychological or forensic testing), or a master's level therapist. These include licensed Marriage and Family Therapists (LMFTs), Licensed Clinical Social Workers (LCSW), Licensed Mental Health Counselors (LPC), etc[2]. Hypnotherapists and coaches may or may not be licensed—these designations may or may not require certification. The same may apply to clergy or spiritual-based counselors, or yoga teachers. Make sure that you know the level of credentials the person you are considering working with has. Insurance companies will usually require a professional license to pay for services (more on insurance and in-network versus out-of-network therapists ahead). Unless there are compelling reasons otherwise, you will want to work with a licensed/certified professional.

Find providers that specialize in the issues you are seeking help for.

Specialty treatment can be an important consideration for a positive outcome. Not all therapists treat all conditions. The level of training and experience that is necessary to do effective therapy is enormous. If you go to a therapist who is not experienced or properly trained, you will likely not progress. In fact, there are conditions including eating disorders, trauma, or obsessive-compulsive disorder (OCD) that, if improperly treated, can actually become worse. A good therapist should refer you to a specialist if they do not do the kind

---

2   letters may vary between states

of work you need. Sometimes, a versatile therapist can use various approaches and methods depending on the situation at hand. This is great, if the therapist has the proper training and experience to do effective work. Always ask about specific specialty training.

Here are some questions you may want to ask a prospective therapist prior to making the first appointment. This first conversation will give you important information to determine if it makes sense to proceed with scheduling an appointment:

- What is your experience, training, and background in the condition I am seeking help for?
- What is your therapeutic approach and your treatment philosophy?
- How do you handle insurance, billing, and financial considerations (see more below)?

The answers to these questions are important. So is how you feel about how they are addressed. Do you like how the therapist sounds on the phone? Would you want to speak further with him or her? Can you communicate with the therapist directly, or must you talk with an intake person to make the initial appointment? These factors set the tone for future experiences with that therapist going forward, so pay attention to how you feel in this beginning phase.

Understand specialty approaches to therapy and consider expert advice (EA).

The following are some of the more widely used approaches to therapy and specialty treatment options that are available. Whenever possible, we have included expert advice related to their particular areas of specialty. Ask yourself which methods appeal to you or would likely be helpful for your needs. This will help you obtain the proper assistance.

- Cognitive Behavioral Therapy (CBT)
- Dialectical Behavioral Therapy (DBT)
- Trauma Based and Trauma Informed Therapy
- Insight Oriented and Supportive Psychotherapy
- Family Therapy, Marriage, and Relationship Counseling
- Substance Abuse and Addictions Treatment
- Grief, Loss, and Bereavement Counseling
- Child and Play Therapy
- Eating Disorders Treatment
- Gender Specialist
- Neurofeedback
- Neuropsychological Testing
- Art Therapy, Music Therapy, Equine, or Animal-Based Therapy
- Hypnotherapy
- AA and Twelve-Step Programs
- Yoga and Meditation as Therapy

——— *Cognitive Behavioral Therapy (CBT)* ———

Cognitive Behavioral Therapy was developed in the 1980s as a targeted treatment for depression. It is also very beneficial for anxiety disorders. This type of therapy focuses on identifying, challenging, and changing unhelpful thoughts, beliefs, and attitudes. These 'cognitive distortions" and the problematic behaviors that result from distorted ways of thinking are the focal point of this type of treatment. CBT is excellent for dealing directly with phobias and anxiety-based avoidance, using exposure therapy. Treatment usually targets current here and now problems. CBT has a lot of clinical research demonstrating evidence for success. The book *Feeling Good* by Dr. David Burns is highly recommended for this type of therapy. Many useful CBT workbooks are widely available for kids, teens, and adults. CBT is usually a shorter-term approach and sometimes involves a predetermined number of sessions (which may be revised) that are agreed upon at the start of therapy.

—————— *Dialectical Behavioral Therapy (DBT)* ——————

Developed by Marsha Linehan in the late 1980s, dialectical behavioral therapy teaches essential self-regulation and management skills. DBT is usually taught in four modules: mindfulness, emotional regulation, distress tolerance, and interpersonal effectiveness. This can be taught in an individual therapy format but is also very effective in group settings and can involve family training. This method of treatment is highly effective for people who struggle with strong emotions and behaviors, because gaining coping and life skills to regulate powerful emotions can reduce negative behaviors. Family training empowers parents and loved ones and has been clinically proven to help with issues of self-harm/cutting, suicidal thinking or behaviors, acting out or acting in, and in instances where hospitalization has happened or are at risk to occur.

Dr. Laura Richardson, Ph.D. is a licensed psychologist located in Midland Park, New Jersey who specializes in DBT and trauma-based therapy (which focuses on resolving traumatic experiences). Dr. Richardson feels passionately about DBT treatment because she believes it really works: *"The advantage of being treated by a well-trained specialist is that these methods get to the heart of the issue and teach the proper skills to deal with symptoms. DBT stabilizes behavior in an effective and targeted way."*

According to Dr. Richardson, professionals who are highly trained in DBT provide the most targeted and effective treatment available for borderline personality disorder, bipolar disorder, and other mood dysregulation disorders. Laura advises clients to *"find the correct person to do the appropriate therapy because not all types of therapy treat everything. Be clear about the problem that you are trying to solve and find a good therapist that is specialized to work with that condition. Also, know that there is hope. People used to think that patients with borderline personality disorder or those who were suicidal or who self-harmed were hopeless. The truth is quite the opposite. With the correct treatment, people with these conditions can do well. DBT and trauma therapies can be life changing."*

─────── *Trauma-Based and Trauma-Informed Therapy* ───────

Psychological trauma is emotional or mental damage that may occur as a result of a severely distressing event(s). Trauma is understood to lie in the eye of the beholder, meaning that each person interprets life events differently. What may or may not be experienced as traumatic will depend on the individual who has experienced it. Dr. Bruce Friedman, who is interviewed in depth in the chapter on medication, has shared that he believes trauma can behave like a "big masquerader." This means that trauma can express itself as other mental health conditions, such as anxiety or depression, and not only as post-traumatic stress disorder (PTSD). Most mental health professionals understand the devastating role trauma can play in the life of someone who has gone through it, but not all therapists are trained to effectively work with it.

The central nervous system controls and regulates many aspects of basic human functioning. Sometimes the CNS gets stuck in a groove, so to speak, especially when trauma is involved, and can contribute to states of heightened anxiety or depression. **Polyvagal Theory**, coined by Stephen Porges, looks at the vagus nerve (not Las Vegas) and central nervous system reactions to perceived life challenges. According to this neurologically based perspective, we can actually map and interact with our autonomic nervous system to learn to regulate and direct ourselves toward a more desirable state. This involves amazing, cutting-edge neurobiology, and we can all learn this. We each have the ability to understand and alter our "neuroception" responses. A therapist can teach this, but this is also something we can learn and practice on our own. How cool is that?

However, Dr. Richardson emphasizes that complicated trauma symptoms are best treated by a clinician who is either a trauma specialist or, at the very least, trauma informed. Otherwise, symptoms can actually get worse. Laura utilizes techniques called eye-movement desensitization reprocessing (EMDR) and dialectical behavioral therapy- prolonged exposure (DBT-PE), which are proven and effective methods for safely dealing with trauma. Other forms of validated trauma therapy also exist. If you are interested in this type of treatment, take some time to research the methods used by the therapist you are considering. This can often be a fast and effective way to move Krazy forward if trauma is a factor.

Insight-Oriented and Supportive Psychotherapy

Insight-oriented and supportive psychotherapy is the pioneer model of talk therapy. First introduced by Dr. Sigmund Freud around 1900, psychoanalysis was the first type of medical treatment where a patient would "talk out" what was going on in their mind. Using free association, dream analysis, and revealing human drives through transference onto the analyst, core issues are thought to emerge. These patterns can then be interpreted by the analyst and are used to resolve internal conflicts. This basic model of therapy has been substantially refined over the years. Many brilliant, thoughtful, and groundbreaking psychiatrists, psychologists, and psychotherapists have contributed new angles on this basic structure over the years. In the 1940s, person- or client-centered therapy, attributed to Carl Rogers, recognized a need for the therapist to have "unconditional positive regard" for their client.

Do you want to know the "why" of what is going on inside you? This is insight. Receive warm and nurturing support from your therapist as you talk out your concerns? This is unconditional positive regard. These factors are, and always will be, essential elements in therapy.

Even in specialty treatment where techniques are the primary focus, safety and support will always be the cornerstone and foundational base of a successful therapy relationship.

Family Therapy, Marriage, and Relationship Counseling

Ah, family therapy. This clinical orientation has been at the heart and backbone of my professional life. I have been licensed as a marriage and family therapist (MFT) in three different states. I sat on the state board that first created professional licensure for MFTs in Alaska. MFTs are extensively trained to work with individuals, couples, and families to promote healthier relationships. By including our most influential people in therapy with us, we can all be part of the solution, and learn valuable life and relationship skills together.

Family systems theory was first developed in the 1950s by such visionaries as Virginia Satir, Jay Haley, and Murray Bowen, among others. This distinct branch of therapy stood on the shoulders of many community-based original family therapists, such as chiefs, clergy, or physicians. As the discipline of family therapy has grown, it has also evolved into a highly specialized form of treatment. For example, relational life therapy (RLT) was created by the amazingly talented Terry Real. In my opinion, RLT is the most effective form of marriage or couples counseling available today. The results that can be achieved with RLT are unlike any other form of relationship counseling. Family therapy is also a necessary part of treatment, in the opinion of most professionals, when working with children or teens. It is recommended for addictions, eating disorders, and many other conditions. In fact, I cannot imagine effective therapy for most situations that does not involve educating and empowering parents, family members, or significant others. Confidentiality is an important issue to address at the start of therapy when multiple people are involved, so be sure to ask how this is handled at the very beginning. I simply *love* family therapy and family therapists! 'Nuf said.

———— Substance Abuse and ————
Addictions Treatment

This specialty area focuses on addictions, and how to manage the severe and life-altering effects of alcoholism, drug addiction, and other addictive processes. Most addictions specialists have a CADC or similar credentialing, and specific training in the neurology and medical aspects of addiction and the "disease model." Because the potential for bodily harm is so great, understanding the level of addiction treatment a person needs at any given time is critical. Detox in a medical setting may be a necessary first step before any other work can begin if the level of severity is high.

Lani Bonifacic is bright and bubbly, as generous with her knowledge as she is with her smile. She is a licensed clinical social worker who specializes in Addictions and Grief Counseling. Twice a month, these two areas of study are combined, when she volunteers her time to run a free bereavement support group called "Hope and Healing After an Addiction Death," which she co-founded in 2015.

According to Lani, the importance of working with a specialist in addictions is that they are trained to identify and treat the underlying issues (trauma, anxiety, depression, stress, maladaptive coping skills) that lead a person to misuse and abuse substances. Using evidenced-based studies and techniques, this medical condition can be effectively treated.

Lani emphasizes that *"addiction is a family disease and everyone in the family plays a role and is impacted, thus family therapy is highly recommended. For a loved one, this may involve education about enabling and how to set effective limits and boundaries while focusing on self-care. Families are systems, and when one member changes, all must adjust."*

——————— *Grief, Loss, and* ———————
Bereavement Counseling

Grief can involve the loss of anything relevant to an individual, such as the loss of a loved one, a career, the parting of a relationship, financial status, or physical capabilities. It is important to note that grief is not the same for every person or relationship. When an individual has adaptive coping skills, formal treatment is usually not needed for grief. From her observations, Lani Bonifacic, LCSW notes, *"most people brace themselves the first year after a loss. They anticipate with white knuckles birthdays, holidays, and other significant milestones and rituals. They often feel a sense of relief that they have survived the first year of their loss. But as time passes, it is not uncommon to feel overwhelmed by the unexpected feelings that can emerge in year two, due to their new reality and the permanence of the loss."*

Complicated grief, according to Lani, is when an individual has lost someone or something close to them and has great difficulty integrating that loss into their present life. As a result, they are caught in a cycle of relentless pain that can be paralyzing and substantially affects the ability to function, their relationships, and overall well-being. A person is *stuck* in an ongoing state of despair. Columbia University School of Social Work has a Center for Complicated Grief led by Dr. Katherine Shear, M.D., which trains clinicians to use targeted, evidence-based methods of treatment to help those suffering to become "unstuck." You can learn more by visiting their website at http://complicatedgrief.columbia.edu.

——————— *Child and Play Therapy* ———————

Children are not adults in smaller bodies. Understanding child and adolescent brain development is essential to work with children or teenagers that need help. The level of cognitive and emotional development of a young person must be considered when assessing their behaviors. Treatment should be tailored to the individual state any young person functions within. Traditional talk therapy methods may be valuable for a highly verbal young person, or they may not. Sometimes, other, less verbally oriented approaches may be a better fit for a child who needs help.

Play therapy is a targeted form of psychotherapy that uses art, toys, or other methods to act out internal states of being. Sand play is a wonderful example of this. A large selection of action figures, animals, and other small figurines are made available. A tabletop sand box becomes the stage. Figures are selected, and scenarios are enacted in the sand. Through these psychodramas, issues are visually represented and can be understood and assisted without using many words. I had the opportunity to personally do some sand play therapy before a life-altering event. Using this method, I was able to bypass my judging/thinking mind and simply access my internal feelings. I was amazed by the scenarios I created and what underlying issues came out. I found this to be helpful in a different way than talk therapy usually is. This is only one of the many forms of therapeutic play therapy available that trained child specialists might use.

Parental education and involvement in treatment is most certainly a given when working with children and teenagers. It is important to discuss confidentiality policies prior to starting therapy with multiple family members to ensure that the therapist's philosophy is in line with your own. Confidentiality is necessary to provide the safety of expression that a young person needs to open up in therapy. At the same time, keeping a parent in the loop, and educating them regarding what they should do to help the situation is also imperative. There are ways to allow for both aspects to take place, such as including parents in family therapy sessions and having signed releases in place. Clearly understood policies about confidentiality are always necessary but are especially crucial in adolescent and family therapy.

——————— *Eating Disorders Treatment* ———————

Eating disorders (EDs) are a highly defined specialty area of treatment. There is a good reason for this: There is a high potential for bodily harm or death associated with eating disorders, so there is no room for error.

Dr. Tina Sherry is a licensed clinical psychologist in practice since 2006 in Wyckoff, New Jersey, and eating disorders are her specialty. Dr. Sherry stresses the importance of being treated by a trained specialist for an eating disorder due to the complex medical concerns and complications. *"Proper ED treatment addresses many aspects of a person and often requires a team approach. This may include a trained therapist, a pediatrician/MD, a nutritionist, and in some cases, a psychiatrist. The team should all work together to ensure that a person is medically stable enough to participate in outpatient therapy, and if not, to be able to safely refer him/her to a higher level of care."*

Dr. Sherry goes on to say that due to the current societal emphasis on diet and weight-loss fads, it may take a trained professional to actually spot an eating disorder. *"It can be a slippery slope into disordered eating patterns, and this can arise abruptly, particularly after an activating event. For instance, a physical injury that interrupts a regular exercise routine and causes a person to gain weight, or even a comment about one's weight from a coach or friend, can take root. Once a person begins restricting intake, whether it be total amounts eaten, or types of foods, or times to eat, he/she can get stuck in the vicious cycle of restricting, binge eating, purging, or over-exercising. The longer these behaviors occur, the more ingrained they can become; therefore, early diagnosis and treatment are critical."*

Dr. Sherry uses CBT-E (Cognitive Behavioral Therapy Exposure) in her practice, because it is evidence-based and it treats not just the outward signs of an eating disorder, but also the underlying factors such as poor body image and low self-esteem. *"Treating the symptoms and also the underlying factors of over-evaluation of shape and weight that maintain this disorder are crucial for success. Additionally, family education, support, and involvement are also necessary for a full and complete recovery to occur."*

Gender Specialist

Issues of gender and sexual identity have received a lot of attention lately. The world has undoubtedly become more gender-fluid, and it is increasingly common for people to identify as non-binary or *queer*. At the same time, gender identity issues can be very confusing territory for KGs (maybe we should change this to KP, or KrazyPeeps?) and for those who love them. When the distress associated with these issues becomes overwhelming or is just plain murky, a gender specialist may be helpful.

Rosalie Cespedes is a licensed clinical social worker who practices in Montclair, New Jersey, and is a gender specialist. She says that her role is to assist people in identifying or becoming more comfortable with their gender and issues related to sexuality. *"We are born with a gender identity, but this may not stay the same over time. Our sexuality changes throughout our lives and our gender identity may also change. Gender issues can arise at any age, as young as three or much later on in life. Our personality shifts, and so may our gender identity. A gender specialist can help guide a person to find their own answers to difficult questions, relating to why they feel certain feelings, or if they are normal. These struggles are often very confusing and distressing."*

A gender specialist has specific skills and training to understand and adequately assist a person navigating these confusing, and sometimes controversial, issues, feelings and questions. Such challenges can involve deep shame and confusion, which can lead to isolation, anxiety, or depression if ignored or left untreated. This population has a higher than average risk for self-harm or suicide attempts, which is why proper treatment is vital. Parents sometimes mistakenly believe that paying attention to gender concerns will encourage them. This is a misperception. Do not hesitate to seek out a gender specialist if there are concerns. Rosalie adds, *"Acceptance of ourselves or our loved one, along with a non-judgmental attitude while sifting through these feelings and questions, is essential. It is OK to investigate and take the time to find real answers to these difficult questions. Please love and accept yourself every step of the way. There is nothing permanent except change."*

Neurofeedback

Neurofeedback is a type of physically based treatment that uses real-time brain information via electrodes placed on the head and a screen, like a video game. It is also called biofeedback or neurotherapy. The goal is to access brain wave patterns and train a person to interact with them to self-regulate and alter their own brain functioning. This is more commonly used with attention deficit disorder, although addictions and other mental and emotional conditions are thought to be effectively treated with this method. Some tout the benefits of this method, and others question its validity. There is little conclusive evidence that supports either perspective, but there is no real downside that I know of either. I have had a few patients who have reported good results with neurofeedback, and it was covered by their insurance.

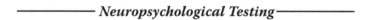

Neuropsychological Testing

Not actually "therapy" per se, neuropsychological testing is a sophisticated method of assessing what is going on inside the brain. This testing is conducted, or interpreted, by a neuropsychologist. It may take many hours or days to complete. The results look at neurology as well as psychology and can provide a concrete diagnosis based on data for many forms of learning disabilities and psychiatric conditions. This can be useful if the diagnosis is not clear or when a rationale for providing accommodations in school must be obtained. This testing can be costly, so look into how billing is handled. In our case, I had both of my kids tested around the ninth grade, and I found the information that was revealed through this process to be invaluable. I was able to get a clear and objective snapshot into how their brains function, and also provide meaningful data-based assistance both academically and emotionally.

Art Therapy, Music Therapy, Equine, or Animal-Based Therapy

These innovative forms of therapy utilize art, music, animals, or other tangible forms of expression or interaction to achieve therapeutic goals. This can be useful if traditional verbal methods are not desirable or preferred. In the case of trauma or autism or if verbal expression is not the best way to achieve goals, these modes of therapy can be life changing. There is extensive clinical evidence supporting the benefits of these hands-on and expressive modalities of treatment.

Hypnotherapy

This usually involves using deep relaxation and directed focus and concentration to achieve desired results. This may include reducing stress, becoming more open to self-improvement goals such as stopping smoking or losing weight, or making past memories more accessible. Using our minds in deliberate ways to create positive change can be a powerful tool, and this may be helpful in a variety of ways. Hypnotherapy is now commonly used in medical environments to manage the pain or anxiety frequently associated with many conditions. Inquire about training, certification, and methods used to ensure the proper fit for your application.

———— *AA and Twelve-Step Programs* ————

Alcoholics Anonymous was the first twelve-step program. AA has now grown into an international fellowship with over two million members. Founded in 1935 by Bill Wilson (the term "friend of Bill" refers to a person in the program) and Bob Smith as a way for alcoholics to come together and support each other. The stated goal of AA is to become and stay sober. This, and all twelve-step programs, use twelve actual steps and twelve traditions to understand and work through the issues and challenges of sobriety. Fellowship is an essential part of twelve-step programs. Sponsorship is a cornerstone of a successful outcome. Very close relationships are formed, and communities of like-minded people provide the well-needed support and connections with each other that long term sobriety requires. There are no dues or fees for meetings, as they run on donations.

There are over thirty-three different kinds of twelve-step programs now available for people wishing to recover from various addictions, compulsive behaviors, or mental health challenges. There are also twelve-step groups that support family members as well. These support groups are not run by professionals, but by those in recovery themselves as a form of service. Twelve-step programs have a high success rate, and many treatment programs use twelve-step programming as a part of their treatment model. There is a growing movement called "Smart Recovery," which is based on CBT/DBT rather than the spiritual base of twelve-step programs. These meetings are not widely available yet. Moderation Management is another alcohol-related self-help movement that educates members about what moderation actually is, and how to achieve this. Additionally, there are now various moderation apps available to help.

———— *Yoga and Meditation* ————

Eastern practices such as yoga and meditation have been the foundation of mental and physical wellness for millions of people for over five thousand years. In many Asian and Eastern cultures, these practices continue to remain a mainstay of health. Here in the west, yoga has gained popularity since the 1960s. Practitioners swear by the therapeutic benefits of yoga and meditation for the body and mind. Courtney is minoring in Contemplative Studies in college and intends to make these practices and principles part of her social work career when working with children. These methods are now widely incorporated into schools as young as Pre-K! Courtney and I swear by the positive, life-altering benefits of a dedicated yoga and meditation practice.

Kelly Soloway, EYRT (five hundred-hour Yoga Alliance certified), is author of *The Yoga Anatomy Coloring Book* and a master teacher and body-worker. She believes that yoga and meditation are transformative on many levels and has dedicated her life to assisting others in understanding and applying the many beneficial aspects of these principles to daily life. Kelly shares that the therapeutic benefits of yoga include, among other things: *"becoming more sensitive to your body, honing your powers of concentration and focus through the postural practice, and being able to put the world on pause while you spend some quality time with yourself. As the body progresses through the postural practice, self-esteem and self-confidence will follow. However, in my opinion, the most significant benefit of all is that over time we can become less reactive to what life hands us. We learn to respond rather than react, and that is priceless."*

Additionally, the practice of meditation has many important benefits. Learning the tools to maintain a calm and peaceful mind, even amid a chaotic world, has immeasurable benefits. Kelly states, *"By training the mind to calmly focus without distraction, we learn to bring clarity to situations that may have seemed overwhelming. We can become more accepting of ourselves and, in turn, of others."*

For people new to yoga and meditation, Kelly recommends the following:

- *Find a local yoga studio and a well-recommended teacher. There is no substitute for a community atmosphere when you are getting started.*
- *We learn to meditate by meditating. Listening to guided meditation can be beneficial at first. If you can find a meditation group, that will also be helpful.*
- *Don't get discouraged, nobody is good at this in the beginning. We get better as we practice.*

I personally recommend—and occasionally teach—basic yoga and meditation techniques in my private practice. I see firsthand how beneficial even a little practice can make in the lives of the people I work with. When people tell me that they can't do yoga because they are not flexible, I explain that we do yoga to *become more flexible in our bodies and in our minds.* From a biophysiological lens, yoga and meditation actually work on shaping the central nervous system in real-time and can also have long-lasting positive neurological effects. The Yoga Sutras, which is the philosophical text of yoga, says in Book 1 Sutra 2: *Yoga Chitta Vritti Nirodha.* This translates to, "Yoga calms the fluctuations of the mind." Indeed, it does. Namaste!

Make sure the therapist's personality, or fit, is a good one for you.

A licensed, experienced, and highly specialized therapist will be of little value to you if you do not connect with them. It doesn't matter what letters are after their names, or how many years of experience they have. If their values are not similar to yours, or you don't feel comfortable talking with them, then they are not the right therapist for you. Not that you will always love your therapist (because good therapy can sometimes be hard), but when starting out, listen to your gut. The right fit will make all the difference in a comfortable and productive therapy experience.

When Courtney began having social issues in seventh grade, I called upon the services of a well-respected therapist in my area. She used art and play techniques, and Courtney liked talking to her. Over time, however, Courtney did not improve. In fact, her condition began to get worse. I started to feel uneasy when meeting with this therapist for family sessions. Even though I am experienced, I questioned my feelings of unease. When my husband also expressed concern, it became clear that her approach and fit were no longer right for our family. So, we switched therapists. The new therapist's specialty was more effective for Courtney's condition, and the fit for our family was also better. Courtney was never hospitalized again after we switched therapists. Please, listen to your instincts and trust your gut. Bad therapy, in my opinion, can be worse than no therapy. With a reluctant or amped up KG if the approach or the fit isn't right the first time, you run the risk of resistance to future therapy attempts. Take your time and do some research. Get referrals from your doctor or friends that have had good results in therapy. Look at reviews online. Speak directly with the provider whenever possible, and ask all the questions you need prior to making the first appointment. This is time well spent.

Consider the appropriate level of care.
Scale up or down as necessary over time.

Therapeutic levels of care, (or the continuum of care), refers to the concept that a person who needs help will benefit the most from the least intensive level of care that will best meet their needs. What this actually means is that we should consider the level of distress or danger a person is in, and what they need at any given point in time in order to become stable, or to improve.

The levels of therapeutic care range from least intensive to most intensive, and people can level up or down this continuum, as is appropriate for their situation. For example, a person in outpatient therapy may come to need intensive outpatient care (IOP) for a period of time, then return to regular outpatient therapy. Or a person in the hospital might step down to day treatment upon discharge, then go into IOP, or outpatient care when they are ready. Levels of care are flexible and should respond to the needs of an individual over time.

Be aware of financial concerns and insurance considerations when considering programs and levels of care. Insurance companies routinely deny services they do not deem to be "medically necessary." Sometimes it is a fight to get insurance to cover what you believe would be most helpful. I have seen well-meaning partners or parents mortgage their home or go into debt to get expensive treatment for their KG, which may or may not have turned out to be effective in the long run. Relapse is a part of recovery (see the chapter on this subject), and sometimes multiple treatments or rounds of therapy are necessary over time to finally achieve wellness. My advice is, as always, to learn as much as you possibly can when assessing the financial, or other costs/benefits of perspective treatment. This is especially true for higher (and therefore) more expensive levels of care. This is difficult to do while in crisis, so you may wish to obtain the services of a treatment placement consultant or educational consultant—see the chapter on school for greater detail—if critical decisions of this type become necessary.

Therapeutic Levels of Care

Here are details on the different levels along the continuum of care:

- Outpatient
- Intensive Outpatient (IOP)
- Day Treatment or Partial Hospitalization (PHP)
- Hospitalization
- Residential Treatment
- Wilderness Programs
- Crisis or Dangerous Situations

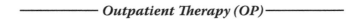

Outpatient Therapy (OP)

Outpatient therapy usually occurs once or twice a week or less, in a private office or agency setting. The frequency and the focus of therapy is up to the individual. This can involve most of the specialties discussed in this chapter.

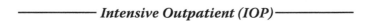

Intensive Outpatient (IOP)

Intensive outpatient therapy usually occurs two to four times a week, for approximately three hours per day, and is frequently conducted in a clinic or agency setting and potentially has virtual options. There are standards regarding time spent to complete an IOP program of usually about nine hours a week for twelve weeks. IOP usually involves theme-based group therapy sessions for substance abuse or mental health issues needing more frequency and intensity than regular OP therapy. Education and training in managing symptoms is usually the focus of this type of treatment, and it tends to last from a few to several or more weeks. IOP can involve medication assessment or management, individual and family therapy, case management, or other customized options depending on the issues that are being treated, and the program selected.

Day Treatment or Partial Hospitalization (PHP)

Day treatment or partial hospitalization (also sometimes referred to as partial care) is much like IOP, but is longer, usually lasting a half to a full day. For kids and teens, there is usually a school component involved, and this is coordinated with the home school, so students do not fall behind. Day treatment offers more therapy sessions, groups, and services in a day, which provides more assistance and support in higher need situations than IOP, but the individual is stable enough to go home at night.

————————— Hospitalization —————————

Hospitalization is when twenty-four-hour care involving skilled medical professionals is required to stabilize a person, deal with a high-level medication situation, or to protect a person from harming themselves or someone else. Hospitalizations are often voluntary but sometimes they are not. Involuntary hospitalization laws vary state by state in the US. Typical length of stay ranges from twenty-four hours to a week at most. Although therapy and medication are addressed to some degree during a hospitalization, the primary goal is to stabilize and move the patient out of the hospital to a lower level of care as quickly as possible.

Discharge planning should begin as soon as the person is admitted; the next steps after hospitalization are actually the most important things to address and obtain while a person is safe. Do not wait for the hospital social worker to create a proper discharge plan for you or KG. You must be very proactive about setting up the best aftercare plan as soon as possible because discharge comes very quickly. The next steps after discharge will become the treatment phase of the Krazy ride.

*————— Residential Care (also see "Therapeutic —————
Boarding and Residential Schools,"
in the chapter on School)*

Residential care involves twenty-four-hour programming, with lots of therapy and specialty types of treatment. This is for those who need longer term and a higher intensity level of care for an extended period (unlike hospitalization, which is brief acute stabilization). The usual length of stay is from three to six weeks and can go up to a year or more in some cases. This level is usually for people who have received many other types of therapy for a long time and are still really struggling. There are many residential treatment programs around the country and beyond that specialize in all types of issues and have different treatment approaches. They can range from bare bones facilities to super fancy rehabs. As with hospitalization, discharge planning is a very important part of residential treatment. The work after residential treatment is over will determine the treatment outcome. It is a well-accepted fact that the longer a treatment resistant person remains in treatment, the better the outcome usually will be. Referrals to transitional living facilities, such as a halfway house, are often made as a step-down component after the residential phase is completed. This can last an additional month to up to a year or more depending on the person and their circumstances.

Lauren Milner, MSW, is a senior treatment placement specialist with many years of clinical and direct placement experience. Lauren shares that *"a person does not have to be fully on board for this level of treatment to be effective, even though these programs are voluntary. Sometimes people go into residential treatment because it is the best-case option, and not necessarily because they want to go. There may be legal, marital, or other compelling reasons to choose to go. However, once there, one may find that it is really helpful and works, even under these circumstances. Do not be afraid to ask questions or ask for help. These illnesses do not discriminate, they affect us all in some way or another. Forget any stigma. Once we begin to open up, we will realize that we are not alone and that help, and hope, are available to us all. I have seen elderly people who have abused alcohol their whole lives finally get well. People who have struggled with an eating disorder for many years enter treatment and change their entire lives. Sometimes we do not know what will click and make the difference at any given point, so never give up hope. Change is always possible!"*

Here are some questions you may want to ask when considering a residential program:

- What is the program treatment philosophy and how long has it been in operation?

- How many therapy sessions are there included weekly, and what type are they (group, individual, family)? Are there specialty therapies such as yoga, body therapies, etc.?
- Is there an individual clinician and family therapist that are consistent throughout treatment?
- If a child or adolescent, how is school incorporated into the program? Academic support? Is there a college prep component, or honors or AP classes?
- What is available for residents during their free time?
- What kind of family involvement is there? Do families come to the facility for therapy if possible, participate in virtual sessions, or are there family weekends or other support?
- Where is the nearest hospital/medical facility? How are medical situations managed?
- What are the financial obligations? Is there a clearly spelled out policy?
- What is the average length of stay? How is this determined?
- How is aftercare and discharge planning conducted?

Wilderness Programs

Wilderness therapy uses traditional therapy techniques in innovative ways. A person is literally transported into a totally new environment, where old ways of functioning can no longer work. Wilderness programs usually involve a certain degree of physical challenge and teamwork embedded within the program experience, and this in and of itself can be transformative. The need to open up quickly, respond to the environment and learn to work with others are all necessary for success in the wilderness. New skills obtained through experiential learning are thought to transfer forward, paving the way for better success at home or in the next phase of treatment.

Outward Bound was the pioneer of this type of wilderness challenge for young people in the 1940s. The concepts of personal responsibility, natural cause and effect, experiential learning and the need to deal with self and others in productive ways make sense. There are numerous wilderness programs available to consider. Not all of them have good reputations, and some are highly controversial. When considering a program, always ensure that they are accredited and that their treatment philosophy aligns with your values and the goals that you are looking to achieve. Get referrals to speak with others who have completed the program you are considering as part of your decision-making process. Upon discharge after the typical six to ten weeks length of stay, participants may return home or be transferred to a Residential Treatment program or a Therapeutic Boarding school.

Courtney went to a wilderness program in Hawaii when she was fourteen. The need for serious intervention was clear after she endured a really bad high school freshman year. We wanted to use that summer to do a total reset. We chose this particular program because of the values they expressed. The benefits of light and air, hard work in an organic garden as a metaphor to also grow on the inside, and natural foods and Hawaiian culture really appealed to us. Some kids go to wilderness programs courtesy of an experienced escort or transportation company, due to concerns of noncompliance or flight risk. Not in Courtney's case. She bought into the need for a reset experience, although none of us had any real idea of what to expect. We got on the plane, landed twelve hours later on the Big Island of Hawaii, and said our goodbyes. I can honestly say that Courtney's seven weeks there were very helpful. She settled down and learned a lot. I do not regret the choice despite the expense (about the cost of a year of college tuition and essentially non-insurance covered). And I know she feels good about her time at PQ. Were all her problems solved? Not by a long shot. In fact, after her next difficult sophomore year, Courtney also went on an Outward Bound Sea kayaking adventure. This experience, although different from PQ, was also helpful but in a completely different way. As you can see, we personally believe in the benefits of wilderness therapy, but it is certainly not for everybody, and it will not solve all of your problems.

A crisis or dangerous situation is unlike any other.

The one and only goal during a crisis is to stabilize the crisis, and averting danger must always be the number one priority. People in crisis do not think clearly, and human neurology will often prevent any logic from occurring. *This is why loved ones must act swiftly on behalf of the person in crisis.* This philosophy must continue until KG is able to regain the ability to think and behave appropriately. Consider this like a snow globe: We need to wait for the glitter to settle before dealing with any other aspect of the situation. The sole focus in a crisis or dangerous situation is to prioritize and ensure safety.

Calling 911, the police, a crisis hotline, or going to the emergency room is the way to go if there is any doubt about safety. Having resources available in advance is also a very helpful strategy if safety is a concern. Do not assume that a person will be OK if you are not sure. This being said, if there is a history of this type of issue, working with your therapist to develop a safety plan that is most appropriate for your particular situation in advance is necessary. Dialectical Behavioral Therapy (DBT) is particularly helpful in averting hospitalizations, so if there is a history of crisis or hospitalization, please consider DBT therapy and a qualified specialist who deals regularly with this.

Understand insurance options and financial aspects.

This is a nasty one. Healthcare in America is a hot button topic that will be sure to inflame any conversation. Mental healthcare sadly falls far behind physical healthcare in terms of accessibility and reimbursement, despite laws that are supposed to prevent this. If you do have insurance, how good is it in terms of real dollars in your pocket?

When it comes to using your insurance for therapy and other covered services, what is the actual rate of reimbursement? Please investigate this in advance whenever possible. You can call your carrier directly, if you have insurance, and find out these answers if you take the time to do this. Then, you can make the most educated decisions possible regarding using insurance for therapy. Some aspects to consider:

- Insurance In-Network
- Insurance Out-Of-Network
- Reasonable and Customary (R+C)
- Insurance Single Case Agreement
- Fee for Service and Sliding Fee Scale

In-Network

Providers have entered into an agreement with one or more insurance companies to provide services to its members at an agreed upon rate. The reimbursement to the provider is usually a fraction of the local going rate. The advantage to the provider is in the referrals they will get from the insured pool who wants to use their services. What they lose in dollars, they make up for in a referral base. Sometimes, treatment needs to be justified in advance to be authorized. Sessions may be doled out to the provider a few at a time. Ongoing paperwork to continue treatment is part of the provider's agreement.

In the case of psychiatry, session times are notoriously quick, and the flavor of the service may not be the same as an out-of-network (OON) provider. A patient once shared an anecdote with me about her experience with an in-network psychiatrist: "I put a Tic Tac in my mouth in the car before I went in. I came back out to my car, and I still had the same Tic Tac in my mouth!" Of course, this is not always the case, and you may get lucky and find a gem. Do your research in advance and keep this potential situation in mind as you seek the quality care that you deserve.

———— *Out-of-Network* ————

Providers have not made an agreement with an insurance company. Their sole relationship is with their patient. If they are licensed and credentialed to provide services, services may be covered under out-of-network (OON) benefits. You will need to know what your out-of-network mental health benefits are, if you have any. You will want to know what your deductible is, which is the amount you must pay before any money will be reimbursed to you. Then find out what percentage of the service they will cover. Specialists who have invested a tremendous amount of time and personal expense to get to the level of expertise that they use in practice are frequently OON. If you have no OON benefits, you can get creative.

———— *Reasonable and Customary (R+C)* ————

This defines what the maximum fee for insurance reimbursement of a particular service can be. This is plan-specific and also depends on the zip code the service is provided in, and also the provider type. For example, in my area, my current fee for a fifty-minute individual or family session is about two hundred twenty-five dollars. This is considered R+C and many insurance plans pay 70-80% of this rate if there are out-of-network benefits available.

———— *Single Case Agreements* ————

SCAs can be made on a case-by-case basis if your insurance company and your provider are both willing. This is a one-time case arrangement where insurance pays your provider their agreed upon fee and treats it like an in-network case for their member (you). Such an agreement must be requested by you, the member, and then be agreed to by your provider. This is a great option to use if you can. You will have to make a good case as to why this particular provider is necessary for you to use over other local in-network options. Be creative and assertive here.

My therapist friend is fluent in Italian, and this was the rationale used to benefit her patient in one single case circumstance, as English was a second language.

——— *Fee for Service and Sliding Fee Scale* ———

This is the fee that is agreed upon between the patient and provider. If a provider is not in-network, they can arrange any fee they wish to with their patient, and sometimes this fee may be negotiated. I have a certain number of reduced fee and very low fee spots available in my practice, and if I wish to work with somebody and the fee is an obstacle, I make my own decisions about this. It does not hurt to inquire, in a respectful manner, if there is any flexibility regarding fees.

Be willing to be honest, dig deep, and work hard. Go all in. Own it, embrace it, work that up-do. You got this!

Therapy is hard work. Yes, you should like your therapist and it should feel good in some ways to address the issues and challenges that have led you to seek help. But the process of looking deep inside and addressing our most difficult things is not always pleasant. This is why willingness to be honest, dig deep, and work hard is the single most important factor in the success of *your therapy*. Therapists do not know everything. It is a collaborative relationship, a two-way street. Be open to their input but listen to your inner truth. The magic is in this collaborative process, which must consist of equal levels of active engagement between both parties in order to work.

   A therapist cannot do anything for anyone that they do not choose for themselves. Developing insight and the ability to apply this knowledge is an act of personal willingness and desire. DBT uses the phrase *willingness versus willfulness* to refer to this dynamic. I always tell anyone I work with that there are two factors necessary for anyone to make any change. The first is ownership of the issue, as in, "yes, this problem is mine to fix." The second is hard work, because change is not an easy process. With personal responsibility and hard work, change will occur. This is where the rubber meets the road.

As we have discussed, not everyone comes to therapy willingly. Sometimes we are beaten and bloodied enough in one way or another that we submit (hitting bottom), and we have no choice but to accept change. Sometimes loved ones push each other into change, so we may reluctantly agree to some degree of change to salvage a relationship. Sometimes a parent acts on behalf of their KG, who is unable to act on their own behalf. However we arrive on the doorstep of potential, I strongly encourage sticking with therapy or treatment until real improvements are made. Change only seeps into our being and becomes a new normal over time, and this can take longer than we like (more on this in the chapter on relapse). Switch therapists, change approaches, or levels of care, if necessary, along the way. The benefits of wellness and personal growth stretch far beyond other riches. The ability to be free, or freer from the ills that plague us, can be nothing short of amazing. The choice to leave KrazyLand is ours alone to make.

Counseling and psychotherapy have evolved in many ways since Sigmund Freud first introduced the concept that our minds and bodies create our personal reality over a hundred years ago. There are so many forms of therapy, specialty treatments, and paths to wellness that are available for any condition. We are fortunate to live in a time where we have these options to help us move towards a less Krazy and more fulfilling life. Please choose to embrace the change that is possible. There is no question that it is a bumpy and sometimes unpredictable KrazyTrain, so hang on tight. The next stop, just up ahead, is health, happiness, and the life that we deserve. We can make this our final stop if we are willing to open up, work hard, and commit to some new ways of living our lives.

CHAPTER 4

Medication: The Deal with the Devil

"There's a little yellow pill . . . She goes running for the shelter of her mother's little Helper. And it helps her on her way, gets her through her busy day."
—Rolling Stones

"Why don't you come with me little girl, on a magic carpet ride"
—Steppenwolf

MARCI

We have an unusual linen closet on the first floor of our house. Although it looks unassuming, it is not your typical linen closet. It has a big padlock on the outside of it. You need a code to gain entry. This is intentional. Early on in our KrazyJourney, it became apparent that we needed a large, secure place in which to store certain things—our block of high-quality kitchen knives, medications, supplements, alcohol.

As our KrazyTrain continued down its uncertain track, a new addition began to grow in this linen closet. Like mold, it was unwelcome. I hid it way in the back of the closet, in the dark. Dangerous. Scary. I call it "the big bag of failed medications." Until now, I am the only one who knows of its existence.

Month after month, this despicable thing grew larger. I have had a love/hate relationship with it. Love, because with each new kid-proof vial came the hope that *this would be the one*. The magic medicine that would calm her anxiety, lift her depression, quiet the voices, focus her attention,

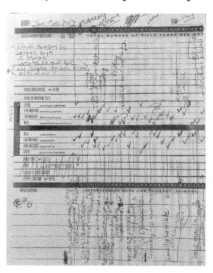

restore normalcy to my girl and to our lives. Hate, because time after time our hopes were dashed. The medicine worked and then did not. There were side effects that were unpleasant, uncomfortable, unacceptable, or intolerable. The exact elements of what was contributing to her Krazy emotions and behaviors became impossible to determine. There was no clear cause and effect. Which medicine did what exactly? I kept charts and graphs. I tracked menstrual cycles, the moon, Mercury in retrograde. I constantly searched for trends or data that would make some sense. Courtney's doctor added new medications which were adjusted, titrated up, titrated down, and eventually discontinued. At one point, Courtney was on a cocktail of *five different medications!* I will never forget the day that she told me that she felt "pixelated." What does that even mean? How the hell did we get here?!

I will never forget the day that medication was first discussed. Courtney was thirteen. She had been cutting for a few months and had recently started seeing a highly recommended therapist. One evening, at the end of a session, her therapist called her dad and me in. She suggested that things were not progressing and thought it was time for us to get a medication evaluation. I was *not* in favor of this. I thought that there was more that could be done in therapy, or with diet and exercise. The therapist pushed the issue; she told me that my own stigma about medication was getting in the way. Feeling ashamed that this could actually be the case, I reluctantly called my trusted colleague, Dr. Bruce Friedman, and set up an appointment.

It is harder than you might imagine to be a long-practicing family therapist and to simultaneously have a mentally unwell child. One may think that it would give me an advantage, or that I would know more about what to do. Yes, on one hand, I have walked with my own patients on the roads that they travel. The vast majority have had positive experiences with medication. It may not be the first one, or the first dose. It is common to have numerous trials. I have told many people in my practice that I see medication like a key in a lock. Once you find the right one(s), it clicks. I honestly believe that this is true, because I have witnessed it time and again. On the other hand, who wants to medicate their child? No one, ever. Right? But here is the cold hard truth: When your kid is suffering, you will do whatever you can do to make it better. It is kind of like making a deal with God (or the Devil). You don't want to medicate, but you are desperate. And hopeful. And scared. You jump . . . and pray . . .

Courtney took her first low dose of Zoloft in mid-October of her freshman year of high school. She had just turned fourteen.

By Halloween, she was refusing to go to school. She became more withdrawn. She talked of a voice in her head telling her to kill herself. I panicked and called Bruce. We raised the dose. At the exact same time, Courtney was diagnosed with mononucleosis, and she came down with a raging full body rash from a previously unknown allergy to the antibiotic she was given for a misdiagnosed sinus infection. The subsequent addition of a strong dose of steroids to bring down the rash was a perfect storm. I watched what looked to me like Courtney on an acid trip, as she watched *Ice Age*, "Mom, the colors . . . " The next night she ran away during a snowstorm in her socks. By late November, she was hospitalized for the first time, for her own safety. *Devastating* is not a strong enough word to describe how bad this experience was. The rabbit hole to hell had opened and swallowed us all alive. Being a therapist did not help at all here. In fact, I felt like more of a failure. While I could obviously help so many others, I was completely unable to help my own kid when she needed me the most.

Since this is the chapter on medication, I will stick to the subject at hand. As I have said, I have a *very personal* love/hate relationship with medication. Looking back, I believe that some of the medications she took actually made things much worse. Whether it is going on, going up, going off, each change completely sucks. At the same time, when you, or someone you love, is such a mess that self-harm is a probability, I am glad that there are medications and knowledgeable providers available that can help us get to another place.

There is no doubt that psychiatric medications have assisted many people with debilitating mental illnesses to live greatly improved lives. I cannot imagine that Courtney would be where she is today without medication. She currently takes a cocktail that helps her a lot and has very few side effects. I am so incredibly grateful for this stability. We still tweak her meds on occasion, and I try to reduce what I can whenever possible. Will she be on these meds forever? I sincerely hope not. Yet, I would not trade where she, and therefore we, are for anything in the world. In terms of quality of life, growth, happiness, and fulfilling her potential, I am extremely grateful. Love/hate.

There are also things that I wish I understood at the beginning of our medication journey. For example, I did not grasp the highly addictive nature of benzodiazepines and how absolutely terrible the withdrawal symptoms are when one wants to reduce or discontinue the dosage. Valium, Xanax, Ativan, and Klonopin can quickly and quite effectively reduce symptoms of anxiety; however, they are also highly addictive. Dependence develops within a few weeks of regular use. There are those who believe that benzodiazepines are the new opioids, in terms of crisis in this country. If regular use has already occurred, make sure the taper down is *very, very slow*. Be very careful with this class of drugs. There is no free lunch. Selective Serotonin Reuptake Inhibitors (SSRIs) can be incredibly helpful in managing the symptoms of anxiety and depression and are non-addictive. However, this class of medication can also cause symptoms of "activation" in younger people (that can present as increased agitation, cutting, or suicidal thoughts), usually within the first weeks of use. This is why there is a "black box" warning for SSRIs and other medications when used with children, teens, and young adults. Does this warning mean do not use these medications when warranted and under the appropriate circumstances? No, not at all. It means watch carefully for any negative changes in mood or behavior, especially in the beginning of use. We must be our own best educated consumers and advocates. As always, trust your instincts. Pay attention. Believe in yourself and listen carefully when something inside you needs to be heard.

This has been my experience as a therapist and more importantly a mom, on this Krazy Krazy Road. But Courtney has been the one who lives this each and every day of her life, so this is really her story to tell.

COURTNEY

To understand how I became as happy and healthy as I am today, we should look back, because this has not always been the case. I was a hot mess for a long time. There are many things that I did, and continue to do daily, which keep me in a balanced and positive mental mind frame. This includes taking my medication. My medication journey has not been an easy one. I have tried a whole pharmacy's worth of medications to find the right combination that finally worked for me. Medication has been an aspect of my life which has made me quite uncomfortable until recently, but at this point I am fine discussing it. Especially if it will help anyone else who is struggling with their mental health.

My journey with medication started when I was a freshman in high school. I started to have suicidal thoughts and I even had a plan to kill myself. I told my therapist, and then my parents, about the way that I was feeling. Concerned, my mother made an appointment with a psychiatrist she trusted, Dr. Bruce Friedman. Bruce would go on to be one of the most helpful people in treating my mental illness. He first put me on Zoloft, a common SSRI (Selective Serotonin Reuptake Inhibitor). Within the first few days of taking it, I became an even more unstable mess. I specifically remember a night where I was sitting on the couch with my mom watching the movie *Ice Age*. I had just started Zoloft, and at the same time was diagnosed with mono and put on steroids for a bad rash I had developed. I remember watching the movie, but I was actually out of my mind—laughing hysterically at things that were barely even funny. This freaked my mom out, because it seemed that the medications made me "too high." She called it a trip. After explaining the situation to Bruce, he changed my medication. This seemed to make things worse, because I soon wound up in the hospital for the first time. I was hospitalized three more times within the next few months, and when not in the hospital I was in a treatment program. Every time I was admitted to the hospital, my medications were changed or adjusted. Nothing seemed to help, and my life just seemed to spin out of control.

I cannot even begin to tell you how many times I made a medication adjustment throughout high school. Each time I hoped it would change the way my mental illness was taking over and ruining my life. With each difference, whether it be the dosage or the medication itself, I thought to myself, "This is going to be it. This is going to be *the one*." Little did I know, we would not find *the ones* until several years later. I'm still not even sure that the combo that I am on now is *the one*, although it is pretty good. I am so much better now than I have been since Krazy took over my life.

For a long time, I felt like I was a test subject, a rat in a maze, with psychologists and psychiatrists analyzing every move I made. If you have ever felt like this, please know that you are not alone. It can take a long time until you find the medication (or combination) that is just right for you. I unfortunately needed a lot of adjustments to finally get it right, which was completely frustrating to say the least. I do believe that all the changes are worth it once you have found the right medication for you. If you are considering trying medication, I can share that they usually are very helpful. In fact, a lot of my friends take something without any problems. If you are on medication and it is working for you, that is fabulous. If that is not the case, I know it is difficult and I encourage you to keep on trying. Have strength and courage. It is not easy, I know this, but I believe that it is worth it in the end.

Even with the right medication, I still must work at dealing with the stuff that my KrazyGirl brain can bring up. As happy as I am, I still face anxiety of one kind or another much more than I would like. These flashes of anxiety do not mean that I should take a Klonopin to calm me down each time I feel upset. In fact, I believe just the opposite. Medication can work to help your body and brain become more balanced. However, when situations arise, as they always will, you need to be prepared. Have an effective list of skills on hand to help you cope. Do not wait until the moment comes when you need the list. Practice these skills before you need them, so you know what to do when the time comes. Personally, I keep a list of my favorite DBT skills in a note on my phone. I am always checking it and adding to it. This list helps me stay more level when difficult situations arise. I do not let my anxious brain throw me off track like I used to. I expect that this will occur, and I am ready!

When discussing medications, I think it is also important to talk about self-medicating. You may think that dabbling around with alcohol or drugs is fun, cool, or helps the pain go away. Unfortunately, I can tell you from my own experience this does not work. Using substances that are not directly prescribed for you will not do anything to help you feel better and can lead you into a terrible place. Sure, taking a puff of a cigarette or vape pen here and there may *seem* to relieve your stress (for a whopping total of two seconds, if that). But when you come back to reality, your problems will still be there. It is the same for alcohol and other street drugs. I would highly recommend staying away from these substances altogether. Self-medicating to distract yourself from what you are feeling will not work and can really hurt you in the future. I have too many friends who have been through so much with addiction. Some have lost their lives. Dealing with an addiction on top of a mental health issue is even worse, because you will have to get clean before you can even begin to get to the root of what your problems are. Please, avoid this at all costs.

As I mentioned before, going through the process of finding the right medication(s) can be a long and painstaking process, but the final destination is well worth it. Throughout this journey, there will be ups and downs, and there may be some roadblocks. One of these roadblocks may be some negative side effects that can come from the medication. These can consist of physical or mental effects ranging from an upset stomach or a headache to mania or full-blown Krazy! Side effects can be extremely unpleasant and turn us off from meds entirely; however, dealing with side effects can be part of the process of finding the correct medication. The key is to not give up. The truth is, most people hit the right medication the first time, with little or no side effects. For me, unfortunately, it took almost four years. It all depends on your body chemistry, your personal issues, and some degree of luck.

To be frank, I would never be where I am now in my life without the experiences I have been through and the medications that I take. I often wonder where and who I would be if I never went on any medication. I do not think I would be where I am today, for good or bad, and for me that is OK. I am aware that my brain chemistry is, and may always be, somewhat wonky. I believe I need certain medications to help level me out, at least right now. One day in the future, I hope to come off my medications, slowly, one by one. But for now, I am content with who I am. I like what I am doing and the path that I am on. Medication can be a difficult aspect of mental wellness. I promise that if you are open minded and honest, consult with good professionals, and do your best to stay level and in the present, then everything else will fall into place.

Creating a positive medication experience involves planning.

Here is our personal, hard-earned advice regarding the use of psychiatric medications:

- **Psychiatrists almost never do psychotherapy these days.** They are medical doctors who prescribe medicine. The same is true for most other medication prescribers. For therapy, see a therapist. The prescriber is there to evaluate and treat with medications

- **Try everything else you can before medication whenever possible.** One you start down the medication rabbit hole it can be hard to go back. This is not good or bad, but typical. Going off meds is hard.

- **Medication can be very helpful, but there is no free ride.** Cost/benefit ratios must be carefully considered and regularly reviewed. Be empowered to direct your medication journey.

- **There are integrative prescribers** that use testing to evaluate the condition, and treat with a hybrid approach of supplements, nutrition, and pharmaceuticals, but they are few and far between, and usually never in network.

- **Track dose, mood, and other factors** (sleep, menstrual cycle, etc.) using a journal, chart, or app. If you can start tracking mood, sleep, etc. *before* starting meds, this is wonderful. Over time, this information will be very helpful. Day to day we can get "lost in the sauce," so to speak. Objective data will be most helpful when evaluating the effectiveness of meds or other deliberate changes. Our perspective can become murky during KrazyTimes, so take the time to do this. You will be glad you did.

- **Pay attention to changes, both positive and negative**. Note them on your mood tracking method. Try to be descriptive and objective when recording data.

- **Watch out for side effects and adverse effects.** They are real and can be seriously problematic. Discuss them with your prescriber.

- **Keep other support in place**. Use medication along with therapy to get the best results. Outcome studies repeatedly cite the best benefits come from medication along with good psychotherapy.

- **Discuss generic options,** pre-authorization, and continuing authorizations with your trusted pharmacist, who will be an important ally on your medication journey. Consider the most economical way to fill prescriptions once medications and dosage are established. Look into coupons, mail order, etc.

- **Be super consistent regarding the dosing schedule**, timing, and food requirements. Inconsistency or missing doses creates imbalances, which we wish to avoid.

- **Make sure you trust your prescriber and have open and honest communication**. They cannot help you if they do not have the full picture. Tell them everything, every time.

- **If you have a team of professionals**, make sure they communicate with each other and are on the same page, especially at times of transition or challenge. I would write group emails to the psychiatrist, therapist, and school contact a lot during hard times.

- **Trust your instincts and listen to your gut;** if something feels wrong it probably is.

- **Do NOT discontinue your meds when you feel better**, or without much preparation. If you are progressing in treatment and wish to decrease or discontinue your medication, plan to reduce slowly. Ensure you keep, or even increase, your other support systems during this process. Do not sabotage the progress you have worked so hard to achieve once you are feeling better. Slow and steady wins the race.

I wish that the use of psychiatric medications was an exact science rather than an art/science hybrid. Someday there will be tests that will precisely pinpoint diagnosis and effective treatment options. This day cannot come soon enough. *Bring it!* Currently, there are genetic testing options that do reveal certain things that may be helpful in considering medications. A company called GeneSight, among others, offers a cheek swab that shows certain gene mutations and metabolic patterns that can affect our mental health. This information can also help predict how we may respond to various medications. For example, the test can reveal if we methylate (a medical term for how our bodies use) our folate or would benefit from supplementation. It reveals if we rapidly metabolize (process) a medication, and therefore need higher dosing; or the opposite and would benefit from micro-dosing. Courtney has had this test done (twice, an older and a newer version), and our trusted psychiatrist Bruce does consider the results to some degree in his treatment algorithm. There are other medical professionals who believe these results are not substantive or helpful when considering medication options. At this point on our KrazyRoad, I believe that more information is better, so I am glad we utilized GeneSight. The last medication Courtney tried is in the red zone, or use with caution, category. It actually did the trick, and was probably about medication trial number twenty-six. It is essentially off the market now due to weight gain class action lawsuits and other nasty side effects. But this medication has actually been the most helpful of all the KrazyMeds we have tried! If you are interested in something like GeneSight, insurance may cover all or part of the expense. Make sure to check in advance and ask your provider about what they find most helpful.

There's a lot to consider when it comes to insurance and medication. It's not easy to navigate insurance, finances, and options for selecting your providers. If you have health insurance, of course you want to be able to use it. However, depending on where you live in the US or beyond, the pool of acceptable and available in-network providers may be slim pickings. Great doctors and providers of all kinds may not want to work directly for insurance companies. This unwillingness is due, in part, to the low reimbursement rates and red tape and paperwork that may be required. Depending on how things go, the first prescribed medication may work well, and you will only need to see the prescriber (psychiatrist, neurologist, primary care doc, nurse practitioner, physician assistant, pediatrician, etc.) every few months. In more complicated cases, you may need to see your prescriber much more often. So the cost/benefit ratio of affordability, availability, desirability, and compatibility will all need to be carefully considered. I hear first-hand from parents, beloved KGs and my patients how difficult it is to strike this balance. Keep in mind that child and adolescent practitioners are usually harder to find than adult providers.

I wish that high quality, affordable, and accessible mental health care was much more readily available to us all. However, you may need to be creative and think outside the box. For example, sometimes a neurologist may treat some of these conditions and may be more available in-network than a psychiatrist is. Maybe the pediatrician or primary care doctor will be willing to prescribe your medication. Sometimes the best way to access medication quickly is through an intensive outpatient program (IOP). However, in the more complex cases, it is my opinion that there is no substitute for a compassionate and highly competent specialist. There is a difference between *spending money* and *money well spent*. Be smart, creative, resourceful, and open-minded. The right answers will come, and the right people will appear. Do not settle for less, my KrazyPeeps!

EXPERT ADVICE

There are many biologically-based ways to view and treat imbalances that may contribute to or cause mental and emotional issues. We have asked a variety of experts to share their treatment philosophies from a body and mind perspective. Some methods are well accepted and established, while others may be considered cutting edge or alternative. Dr. Bruce Friedman is a psychiatrist, Donna Galarza is a functional medicine nutritionist, Dr. Edward Barbarito is a gastroenterologist and Dr. Sheila Newman is a gynecologist. They all view the body/mind connection from different perspectives, and all have their ways and means to assist us when we are struggling. As always, please pay careful attention to your own values and beliefs when considering the best strategies for your own particular situation.

We are so pleased to share this in-depth conversation with Dr. Bruce Friedman. You have heard a lot about Bruce in this book because he is our personal psychiatrist and we feel so fortunate to be able to work with him. Because access to a top-notch New York Metropolitan area psychiatrist is not readily available to everyone, we have elected to include his interview in its entirety:

──────────── *Psychiatric Approach* ────────────

Dr. Bruce Friedman is a board-certified psychiatrist and has a highly successful private practice located outside of New York City. Although he sees adults as old as sixty-five, ninety percent of his practice consists of adolescents and children. I have been professionally acquainted with Bruce (as we affectionately refer to him) for many years. I have collaborated with him and referred many patients to him with great success. When trouble began brewing in the Ober household, I called upon Bruce for assistance. His compassionate and extremely competent care has been invaluable to us on our road into and out of KrazyLand.

What is most important for a young person or parent considering psychiatric medications to understand?

There are a couple of things that are very important to know. One is that no medication is going to be absolutely perfect. Two, there may be a side effect cost to pay along the way. However, with a very small exception, anything that we do with medication can be undone. So if something is not going as planned, we can always phase it out and remove it from the equation. There doesn't have to be a long-term commitment involved when it comes to psychiatric medications.

Why do you believe in pharmaceutical medications over supplements or natural remedies?

I was trained in the allopathic medical model of FDA-approved medications in the United States, which uses medications that have been tested for safety and efficacy. Allopathic medication and alternative medications are not mutually exclusive. They can be combined. However, my training concentrates on the scientific model, and this is where I have the greatest comfort level. I strongly believe that using psychiatric medications as a tool in treatment can open up many possibilities for other modalities to have greater effectiveness. It helps achieve greater success in therapy, it can help with academics, and it can help people be more successful in their relationships. So successful use of psychiatric medication can open doors to many areas of growth. While at face value it seems like the goal is to reduce unwanted symptoms, the hidden and more important benefit is that medication can help people get back on their path, so that they can grow socially, emotionally, academically, and intellectually.

Are there times that medication should not be utilized?

Yes! This is always an important topic for parents and patients to understand. First, you must have a clear-cut diagnosis. It is important to know if this diagnosis responds well to medication, as some do not. For example, in child and adolescent psychology there is a phenomenon called Oppositional Defiant Disorder (ODD). This is a well-recognized diagnosis that occurs in a notable percentage of the child population. Although ODD is a common diagnosis, it does not respond well to medication. There are other treatments that ODD does respond well to, including behavioral therapy and a rewards system. In the case of

ODD, medication would not be a good option. So when considering medication, it needs to be clinically appropriate and known to be helpful for the condition being treated.

How can a teen approach their parents about trying psychiatric medication? What else should be considered in providing assistance to children and teens?

Every teen and parent have their own unique relationship. There are no one-size-fits-all recommendations when it comes to communication between teens and parents. Talking about their feelings is probably the most important part of this communication. It may be helpful to approach their parents and describe, using simple but descriptive words, the feelings that they are experiencing. For example, 'I have been feeling uncontrollable sadness for five weeks,' or 'I have had really bad anxiety and worries that won't go away, despite my best efforts, for about three months now.' Hopefully, this will connect with a parent who is willing to listen and respond to their child's distress. If a parent is open, a typical first step would be to see the pediatrician and to verify that whatever symptoms are occurring do not have a basis in a biological illness. For example, a thyroid disorder could create symptoms of sedation, fatigue, anxiety, or agitation. Mononucleosis can also cause fatigue. Once a medical explanation is ruled out, then a referral to a therapist or psychiatrist makes sense.

It is important to look at biology, psychology (emotions and thoughts), and sociology (family dynamics, friendships, and other social groups) when understanding what is going on with a child or teen. Additionally, if there are other professionals involved, it is very important for all to collaborate and communicate with each other. It may be as simple as a three-sentence email or a one-minute voicemail, but we all must work together and be on the same team. Whether we are coming from the approach of the pediatrician, the psychotherapist, the psychologist, the educator, the family therapist, or the psychiatrist, we all need to be talking with each other and making sure that we have the same common goals in mind. In this way, we can best contribute to the growth and development of the person we are working to help.

What is the youngest age that medication can be used?

It is understandable to be hesitant when it comes to children and using psychiatric medications. I will start medication, if warranted, with children as young as five years old and in very rare cases as young as four. If a parent is reluctant to use medications, I would hope that they would be motivated to try other helpful modalities that are available. These may include psychotherapy, behavioral interventions, nutritional interventions, movement and exercise, and other approaches. If the concerning issues are not resolved with those methods, then it may be appropriate to consider medication.

What are your favorite medications to use as a first line treatment for anxiety and depression in teens and young adults?

I do have a favorite class of medications, which are the Selective Serotonin Reuptake Inhibitors (SSRIs). SSRIs have been approved for use in the United States since 1986, when Prozac first came to market. There are a lot of newer drugs in this class now and they all can be very effective. When picking a medication, we can look for any 'desirable side effects' we want. For example, if a person is lethargic, we can pick a medication that has a side effect of added energy. If somebody has elevated states of agitation, we would want a medication that slows them down and helps them feel more relaxed, so they can sleep at night. The SSRIs are certainly the first line, and probably the best available treatment for anxiety and depression in children and adolescents. They are effective, well-tolerated, and not addictive.

What other advice do you have for teens and parents struggling with mental health challenges?

Be patient. None of these conditions are solved with a magic pill, and none of them are solved overnight. All these conditions take time to develop and also take time to respond to treatment. I typically measure time in weeks and months, certainly not in hours or days. Another thing to keep in mind, is the idea of 'start low and go slow,' relating to medication adjustments. Children's brains are not fully developed until about the age of twenty-five. Therefore, we must be aware that too high of a dose will certainly cause problematic side effects. This can scare the patient, causing them to flee from treatment. A gradual and gentle introduction to medication, with slow adjustments along the way, is a far safer and ultimately more valuable approach. Additionally, using medication along with therapy provides the best clinically proven treatment outcome.

Dr. Friedman is an amazing and highly respected psychiatrist, and his advice is certainly appreciated. In addition to psychiatry, there are also other professional perspectives and treatment options we may choose to consider. Here are some other schools of thought regarding biology and the mind/body connection.

———————— *Nutritional Approach* ————————

Donna Galarza, CN, is a Licensed Functional Integrative Medical Nutritionist, practicing for thirty years in Montville, New Jersey. Donna treats physical and mental conditions from a holistic nutritional approach. This is a radically different approach from the allopathic view, but many are considering these cutting-edge models, especially if they want to avoid psychiatric medications if possible.

Donna believes that *food is medicine*. She teaches that conditions of the mind and body can, and should, be treated nutritionally. According to Donna, the entire body's physical response involves chemicals and hormones. Food and supplementation can change these chemicals and hormones, thus altering the balance of the body and brain. She stresses that this approach is the most natural and effective way to work with many conditions of the body and the mind, both neurologic and psychiatric.

Donna uses sophisticated blood testing and the results of these tests to pinpoint and treat exactly what is going on in the body. Testing may involve identifying toxins such as food allergies, heavy metals, bacteria, yeast, or other pathogens. Tests also search for deficiencies that can manifest as common mental conditions, such as anxiety, depression, attention, or behavioral problems. She goes on to say that getting to the root cause of the problem is essential—if the problem is neurological rather than psychiatric, then medications will only serve to mask symptoms or will not work at all. *"Based on the results of the tests I have ordered to determine the root cause of the problem, I will add in what is missing and beneficial, and/or identify and remove what may be triggering or toxic within the body. This information will be used to create an individualized plan to achieve wellness and balance."*

For a person wishing to become healthier from the perspective of functional or integrative nutrition, the three most important things that Donna recommends considering trying are:

- *Eat a cleaner, more plant-based diet. Eat organic whenever possible. Nutritionally, today's food is nothing like food of the past. To have the nutritional value of the foods of the 1940s, you must eat organic.*
- *Eat lots of antioxidants to reduce inflammation. Fruits and veggies are your best source.*
- *She recommends an elimination diet, in conjunction with a food diary to track your body's response to specific food groups. Some common groups to consider may be dairy, gluten, or any suspected culprit. See if this makes a difference. Eliminate one at a time and give it a month for each trial to determine if it is helpful to your condition.*

Gastroenterologist Approach

Another important perspective comes from **Dr. Edward Barbarito**, a Board-certified Gastroenterologist, Internal Medicine doctor, and certified Therapeutic Endoscopist serving the New York area. Courtney and I sat down with Dr. Barbarito to have a conversation about his thoughts on a subject that has gained a lot of attention lately: the Gut/Mind connection.

He is quite passionate about this subject, having had a near death experience related to his own challenges with gut health. He recovered and is now eager to assist others with his vast personal knowledge and professional expertise. He has a bright and positive energy that is infectious.

Dr. Barbarito tells us that seventy percent of our body's nerve cells live in the gut, therefore the gut is our second brain (or maybe even our first). The adage "listen to your gut" has real truth in it! He sees a strong connection between those with GI issues and mental health challenges, which is an example of the gut/brain connection at work. Which came first, the chicken or the egg? It is unclear currently. This cutting-edge science is just beginning to be understood and not all physicians subscribe to these principles . . . yet.

At least fifty percent of my practice involves patients with IBS (irritable bowel syndrome), diarrhea, constipation, gas, abdominal pain. In the past those patients were thought to have a psychosomatic illness brought on by anxiety: they were essentially blamed for their problems and largely dismissed. Now we know that there is much more to it. There are real physical problems going on that can be creating the anxiety itself. Dysbiosis is a medical term that means bacteria in the gut that is out of balance. This can lead to over or underproduction of serotonin, which is a neurotransmitter that is largely responsible for anxiety and depression symptoms, and for IBS. You are not Krazy, it is not all in your head, this is a real and valid connection.

When asked what he believes can be done to take better care of our gut/brain health, Dr. Barbarito was emphatic about his recommendations. He refers to them as **the four pillars of health**: sleep, movement, proper diet, and mindful attention to mental health, and he strongly believes there can be no wellness without them.

- *Sleep: This is the most important. Protect your sleep by directing patterns of behavior including a good sleep routine, a cold and dark room, and commitment to your sleep as a top priority.*

- *Nutrition: Eat whole and minimally processed foods, and isolate and eliminate irritating foods such as gluten or dairy if you suspect they bother you.*

- *Movement: Do whatever you enjoy, but it must be vigorous and include weight training. Mix it up, keep it fun, but do it!*

- *Mindful attention to your mental health: This includes meditation, yoga, church, therapy, community connection, and anything that gives a sense of purpose and meaning.*

Lastly, Dr. Barbarito suggests that *"we must always apply effort towards the things that we want and be persistent in putting energy into the things that matter to us. We can create much of our own reality by what we chose to focus on, with attention and commitment."*

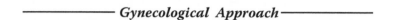

Gynecological Approach

Dr. Sheila Newman is a Board-Certified Gynecologist, practicing for the past twenty-five years in Wayne, New Jersey. Her belief about the role hormones play in the emotional life of a woman is not a straight-line cause and effect dynamic.

Many would like to think that there is a direct link between hormones and mood and would love a magic pill to level that out. The problem with this is that hormone levels change from minute to minute, not just day to day within a monthly cycle. Dr. Newman likens this to looking at a speedometer in a car: It can tell you exactly where you are now, but not where you have been, or where you will be in the future. Rather than hormones being the single culprit for female mood issues, she points to neurotransmitters as an important change agent for modulation of mood. However, she acknowledges that hormones and neurochemicals affect each other, so hormones do play a role. Altering neurochemicals can assist in balancing mood and emotional states, and this definitely interacts with hormones. The question seems to be the age old, what is the chicken, and what is the egg?

Estrogen, progesterone, testosterone, and other hormones are related to many problematic women's health issues such as Pre-Menstrual Dysmorphic Disorder (PMDD). PMDD is a medical condition that can be debilitating and is characterized by extreme and intense mood shifts and

significant physical symptoms such as pain and fatigue.
Symptoms usually subside a few days after the period
comes. The treatment of choice for PMDD is often Fluoxetine
(Prozac), a medicine that alters the neurotransmitter,
serotonin. But a birth control pill called YAZ, which alters
hormones, is also commonly used to treat PMDD. Dr.
Newman points out that, "PMDD can also be helped by
maintaining a healthy body weight and through exercise,
both of which affect hormones and neurochemicals. So, the
root cause of some of these conditions may be hormonal,
but the treatment may not be a straight hormone one.
Balance is the key.

Dr. Newman also recommends that women be proactive regarding their health, and suggests going for all screening tests, practicing safe sex, and learning to love and accept your body. She emphasizes that, "Self-care is not selfish." Now that is a woman after my own heart!

─────── *Yoga and Meditation as Medicine* ───────

Beryl Bender Birch is an American icon. Credited for bringing yoga mainstream in the US in the 1980s, she is the author of *Power Yoga*, *Beyond Power Yoga*, *Boomer Yoga*, and *Yoga for Warriors*. Beryl is my beloved and revered teacher, an activist and visionary. Her energy and passion for self-improvement and compassion for all living beings is evident. She is warm, approachable, generous with her knowledge, and has great wisdom regarding yogic ways to approach mental health and wellness.

All the yoga practices—movement (asana), meditation,
breath work (pranayama), and devotional practices—
are designed to balance the mind and body. Some are
adaptogenic and can be calming or energizing depending
on how they are practiced. Others are primarily calming and

can help to reduce anxiety and hyperarousal, for example. And still others are energizing and can ease depression or boost self-image and self-reliance. It is best to start slowly, experiment, pay attention, and see which practices work best for you.

The Sanskrit word, sattva, in the yoga school of philosophy, means 'light and harmony.' Sattva is one of the three gunas, or qualities of existence, along with rajas (passion, active), and tamas (inertia, inactive). Our yoga practices are designed to help us find balance between hard and soft, active and inactive, effort and ease, and create harmony. Listen to yourself and move toward practices that will help you create a more sattvic state of mind/body balance. Seeking out a certified and experienced yoga therapist to help you find your path can be invaluable.

Beryl also cites the validated therapeutic benefits of these practices for many different health issues and in a great variety of circumstances, such as overall good health, longevity, most anxiety-related disorders, PTSD in veterans, cancer therapy, addiction recovery, weight loss, and numerous others.

There are times and circumstances where other approaches to health and wellness are desirable. The following physical and neurobiological healing modalities are less mainstream in the US but are mainstays of health in Eastern countries such as India and China. East meets West healing is rapidly gaining popularity.

Ayurveda

Ayurvedic medicine is an Indian-based system that focuses on a holistic mind/body approach and is over five thousand years old. It is based on an overall health balancing philosophy but can also address specific health problems. Practitioners look at health through the five elements of space, air, fire, water, and earth. Balancing these elements is a primary goal. Everyone is also thought to possess a basic constitution of mind and body called a Dosha, which can be evened out through nutrition, attention to the emotional state, family relationships, seasonal considerations and other methods to achieve balance and wellness. Most practitioners of Ayurveda do not see this as a substitute for Western medicine under certain circumstances.

Homeopathy

An alternative medicine system developed around 1800, homeopathic medicine uses "remedies" that are prescribed for individual conditions via micro doses of specifically diluted substances. The "Law of Susceptibility" in homeopathy says that a negative state of mind can attract and maintain disease in the body. This is a highly controversial system of treatment and utilization varies widely between regions in the US and countries around the world, but most in the US view this with skepticism.

Traditional Chinese Medicine

Practiced for over three thousand five hundred years, traditional Chinese medicine includes herbal remedies, acupuncture, *qigong* (postural practices), and focuses on *qi* (pronounced *chee*), or energy within the body. Many people that I know personally tout the benefits of acupuncture and *qigong*. I am no expert in these areas, but these are other well-known alternative approaches to achieving balance and wellness within the body and mind.

MARCI

Clearly, there are many ways to view mental health and wellness from a biological and physical perspective. Regarding chemical, nutritional, hormonal, or gut imbalances, how can we know which approach is best for us? In the absence of absolute hard, tangible evidence, the best thing we can do is make our choices based on the information that is available. We must learn all we can, listen to our gut, pun intended, and follow some of the helpful advice shared by those who know a lot about these subjects. Taking personal responsibility to direct our wellness through our lifestyle choices is a theme that every professional has encouraged. There is no downside to these suggestions, and we will surely improve the quality of our lives if we adopt some or all of them.

Although I wonder: Would strict adherence to every possible lifestyle recommendation ever be enough for everyone to avoid or discontinue psych meds entirely? Are the benefits of psychiatric medication worth the costs, literally and figuratively? These are highly personal questions and ultimately, each of us must answer them for ourselves. Aligning yourself with professionals who think as you do will be invaluable.

Please keep in mind that the perspectives shared in this book are the opinions of individual practitioners. I can say with all certainty that other professionals with the same credentials might view these questions in an entirely different light. The viewpoints of anyone you seek assistance from are best seen as a jumping off point, so pay close attention to your own instincts. Do you agree with what is presented to you? Disagree? Are you unsure? Let your own intuition and inner guidance be your number one teacher. Seek your answers and you will find them. I am extremely grateful we live in a time where all these options exist for us to choose from. We are so fortunate to have such a varied menu to pick from to assist us as we travel through KrazyLand.

PART II

IN THE THICK OF IT

CHAPTER 5

The School Years: Krazy Plays Out on a High School Stage

"Well, I did not think the girl could be so cruel.
And I'm never going back to my old school."
—Steely Dan

"You know the world can see us in a way that's
different than who we are."
—Troy, High School Musical

COURTNEY

It is difficult to be a student, period. It is even harder when you are a student who suffers from mental health problems, such as anxiety or depression. This is my story about the experiences I had in school, what helped me, what hurt me, and what I wish I knew when I was going through my hardest times.

I went to a quaint kindergarten through eighth grade public school as a child. I had friends, did well in my classes, and everything was perfectly fine. I was involved in school. I often got the lead in the school plays and played soccer on the town team my dad coached. I went to that school from kindergarten through fifth grade. I had heard the girls at my camp talking about the private schools they went to and it sounded so cool—I wanted this experience. So, I begged my parents to let me transfer to private school.

The next year, in sixth grade, I started at the ABC School of Excellence[3]. At ABC, there was a clear difference in the environment, the academics, the teachers, and, of course, the students. I went from being the smart girl in a small-town school, to being an average, relatively poor girl from a town that nobody had heard of, far away in the woods. This new identity was a big change for me. I had to start over and make a whole new friend group. My insecurities prevented me from easily making friends—I felt awkward and out of place, but I persevered.

Sixth grade was fine, everyone at ABC was getting settled and getting their feet on the ground. Seventh grade was all about forming friend groups and creating cliques. I was in the "popular" group, but this was not easy. I became increasingly aware of the ways the girls stayed so skinny (eat ice chips for lunch), and the expensive clothes they wore, which I did not. Eighth grade was a notable year. I made some bad choices, my "friends" ostracized me from the group, and they went out of their way to make me feel awful about myself. They spread rumors about me and sent me horrible texts. The other group of kids in our grade called "the Bookies" (because they were smart and nerdy) took me in, but although I tried, I didn't feel like I really belonged there. I felt sad and alone. This was around the time I started self-harming regularly, and participating in other self-hating activities. Go figure . . .

A few months after high school began, I felt like I had no friends, and so much anxiety and depression that I refused to go to school. This was fueled by an environment in which most everyone

3   Name changed.

seemed pretentious and judgmental of anyone who was different, no matter what was preached from the morning meeting pulpit about "diversity." I got my first boyfriend and clung onto him like a life raft. Making new friends did not feel like an option after what had occurred the previous school year, and I didn't trust anybody anyway. So, I proceeded to accentuate my differences, isolating myself and dressing all in black.

I had meetings with the high-school guidance counselor. He tried to help me with my social anxiety as much as he could. He gave me advice on how to make more friends and fit in better. But in a way, I did not want to fit in. Being the outcast was the identity I had taken on. I had put myself in a box and I became imprisoned within it. To give you a legitimate visual, imagine a girl in an all-black, Hot Topic outfit, complete with heavy eyeliner and piercings—in a sea of smiling pastel Vineyard Vines. I was still doing well enough academically, as I always did, (hair flip), but I was so uncomfortable and anxious that I shut down from any other activities.

Many of my teachers at the ABC school worked hard. They helped me so much and taught me things I would have never learned otherwise. The academics there were good, and some coached me through some of the most difficult times of my life. Looking back, I wish I was able to accept their help. If you can relate to this or this sounds like you in your school environment, please don't feel like you must run away. Try to open up and accept some help. It really is the better choice. It is awesome to be different. Try to embrace your differences, although I understand how hard it is to do in middle and high school.

As my junior year approached, it became obvious that I needed to change schools. The choice was between transferring to a therapeutic school or attending my local public school. Fortunately, there was a new program that had just been created for kids with anxiety in our local high school called SAIL (Student Attendance in Lakeland) which is where I ended up. Piece of KG advice: if your local public school has a program like this, *try* and choose it over a fully therapeutic school. These transitional programs allow students to integrate into "typical" classes when they are ready and keep the rest of their life as normal as possible. For me, being in public school, even if it was in a secluded corner of the building with only three people in a class, was amazing. I was able to be myself, dress how I wanted, and spend the whole day crying if that's what I needed to do. I felt no judgment from my teachers or peers. I met so many new people, of all different colors, shapes, sizes, styles, sexual orientations, anything I could imagine. It actually felt like an ordinary place to be, and I began to feel more normal within myself.

By the time the year ended, I was thriving in all my classes and had even integrated back into the "typical" classes. I was making new friends, getting my feet back on the ground, and becoming more confident in myself. Here is another piece of advice for you, KG: if you see someone who seems like-minded, go and talk to them, even if it seems SUPER scary! You never know, they may end up becoming your best friend. It feels so much better to go to school when there are people there you can connect with.

My senior year of high school finally arrived, I was in all regular classes, including an AP course. I joined some clubs, went to prom, and even got to sing the national anthem at my high school's graduation! I felt so proud of myself and very deserving of my happiness. It was so nice for me to finish high school on a high note.

College, depending on who you ask, can seem like a fun or a scary thing, maybe even a little of both. For us KGs, going away to a brand-new environment, with a whole new atmosphere, new people, new coursework, *new everything*, can be scary! For me, my first experience away at college was not great. I needed to come back home, regroup, and take things a little slower. This was not easy, and a lot of my old feelings and insecurities returned. This is how life goes, a few steps forward, a few back. That is OK, because I can't imagine that I could be any happier than I am with the life I have right now. I finally feel like I have found my place, my people, and my path. As hard as it all has been, it is worth it to have the life I have now. And I am so happy to get to share this all with you.

Here is some advice if you are getting ready for college: Set up accommodations and your support systems before school starts. You will begin school with less anxiety and more comfort. Also, as weird and annoying as it might sound, going to all those welcoming events in the first week of school can help you get acclimated and begin to make new friends in your new environment. Talk to people who seem like-minded, or those who seem a little different, or who look like they may not be fitting in so easily. They may be more approachable at the beginning of your new adventure. Remember, everyone looks more confident on the outside than they are probably feeling on the inside.

Some school tips, KG to KG:

1. Even if the actual class work seems difficult, do *not* let it get the best of you. Push through and kick ass like you know you can! Get a tutor, make a friend in your class, find a study buddy. Remember, you can do anything you put your mind to. Do you.

2. Friends are always changing and evolving in school, especially in middle and high school. Know that this will get easier and become more stable as time goes on. Hold on to the good people and let go of the toxic ones.

3. Teachers, and professors too, can sometimes be a pain. If you are kind and patient with them, you are doing your part. Be respectful and interested in what they are teaching while in class, and they will probably help you. They may even go the extra mile when you need it most. Be open if you can.

4. Get involved in clubs or activities that seem interesting to you. You will make friends and connections that will make school more fun and a better place to be. Try it!

Finally, keep chugging on, you wild child. You are awesome! I hope this information has helped you better understand what it can be like to journey through school with mental illness and get some tips and tricks on how to make it through those rough days that can feel like they are never going to end. School can feel like an intimidating place, but please be tough and push through the hard times. There is light at the end of the tunnel, and the future that you want and deserve is just up ahead of you.

MARCI

I always hated school as a child. I didn't have friends, did not belong to clubs, didn't participate in activities or in most of my classes. I can't remember much about my early school days except for a few snippets, like frantically ducking under the desk for air raid drills in the 1960s when I lived in Brooklyn. Or falling off the monkey bars and landing flat on my stomach gasping for breath, while the kids on the playground laughed and called me fat when I first moved to New Jersey. I recall cutting classes in junior high and smoking cigarettes in the smelly bathroom stalls. Shortly thereafter I was smoking weed and running away from home. This trajectory ended in my placement in what was then called reform school by my freshman year of high school. I returned for senior year, but rarely attended. School was an unhappy place where other people seemed happy, which only made me feel even more like a loser. I got through those difficult years and by some force of grace, I fell in love with college! I found my place at a small, progressive state school tucked away in the woods. I felt comfortable there, connected with other students and professors, discovered a brand-new love of learning and my lifelong passion for psychology. But those early school years were rough.

When I had children, I was determined that their education would be an entirely different experience for them. Starting in preschool I looked for the best schools possible, carefully considering both the educational environment and social/emotional aspects. Before moving to the rural town we chose when my oldest was entering preschool, I met with the principal of the kindergarten through eighth grade school. I loved her, but sadly she would leave the district later that year. Over the next seven years we had five different principals come and go. This turnover exacerbated the problems and limitations I perceived. When Courtney mentioned going to private school in fifth grade, I figured, why not try it out? She scored well on the placement test, was accepted to a few schools, and was offered a nice scholarship to one of them. We went for it.

Courtney started at the ABC School of Excellence[4], an elite sixth through twelfth grade coeducational school, in sixth grade. We were enthusiastic, so the stressful hour-long commute with awful New Jersey traffic seemed worth it. She wore her uniform with pride (complete with monogram crest), made a bunch of new friends, and seemed to love her teachers, classes and activities. I also drank the Kool-Aid, going to parent functions and serving on various committees in between seeing my therapy patients in my office a few towns away. Every morning, when we drove onto the perfectly manicured twenty-two-acre campus, I beamed as the headmaster enthusiastically waved us into the drop-off area. When a year later, Courtney's older sister was offered a spot as an incoming freshman at ABC (including a scholarship and a place on their varsity soccer team), we were all in. Life seemed great.

Courtney's problems appeared midway through seventh grade. She started having social anxiety and became increasingly perfectionistic. If she got less than an A in anything, she was distraught. We started her in therapy, and life continued along its busy path. But things were not getting better. I will never forget that sunny spring day in eighth grade when I discovered she was cutting herself. I was snooping in her phone and came across a picture of a girl's arm, with about twenty-five thin, perfectly spaced cut marks along the forearm. The thought slowly dawned on me that this was Courtney's arm, and the room around me began to spin. I gained my composure, confronted her, and she admitted that she had been cutting. As shocking as this was, we addressed it in therapy, and I thought the issue was resolved. Courtney was so damn good at hiding her pain.

---

4   Name changed, but not much . . .

Near the end of eighth grade an incident occurred at a sleepover at a friend's house, and Courtney was literally shunned from her friend group. The texts that she received from her closest girlfriends were horrifying. "Slut," "dirty whore," "freak," poured in from those sweet girls she had grown so close to. They stared her down in the hall whispering to each other, while pictures appeared on social media of all the fun activities they were doing together without her. The ancient retiring middle school guidance counselor was no help at all, while the parent of the sleepover night advised me that the girls should just "hug it out." If only it were that easy. Especially since that incident involved her son, two years older, who was at the center of the event. But nobody shunned him—as so often is the case, his life went on uninterrupted. Clearly the rules for boys are still different than they are for girls. I watched as my sweet daughter had her first encounter with darkness.

Middle school graduation could not come soon enough. In retrospect, she should have changed schools at that juncture. But there were fifty new incoming freshmen joining her rising class including her sister, and she had a great summer touring with her rock-n-roll chorus, so we decided to stay the course. Ninth grade began well, but as the leaves began to change, so did Courtney. She started antidepressant medication around Halloween, and unfortunately also contracted mono. This slippery slope became a perfect storm, which led to multiple hospitalizations and treatment programs over that fated freshman year. We were trying our best to keep Courtney alive, as the rabbit hole to hell was swallowing her up.

Krazy, in fact, does play out on a high school stage. The Krazier she became, the more people disappeared, exit stage right. Shame, like a black cloud, billowed off the students, parents, and even some of the faculty members. Their averted eyes and quick avoidance made it seem like her condition was contagious. How does one address the insidious current of judgement on twenty-two perfectly manicured acres? You can't—it quietly sucks you up and takes you down.

We deliberated changing schools for hours, this time with her new therapist, but no option seemed to be a good one even though the ABC School of Excellence was completely ill-equipped to deal with her needs. I would be in the middle of a therapy session twenty minutes away and get a frantic text saying that she was going to walk out into the street and kill herself, or get a call from the school to please come pick her up, right *now*. I would end my session full of apologies and excuses, and frantically race down the highway to get her. I felt like a therapist fraud and a complete parenting failure, running on pure adrenaline while my kid continued to implode.

The point finally came where there was no other choice but to leave. After carefully considering our options, Courtney wound up at our local high school, and that was the best thing that ever could have happened. Despite the frantic search for "the right school," including the option of residential or therapeutic boarding school, the universe smiled upon us. Our district had just launched an innovative new program specially designed to meet her needs. Over time things stabilized, then slowly began to improve. Because of the accommodations and support services Courtney received she was able to find her way back to herself, this time on a different high school stage.

Watching Courtney sing the national anthem at her high school graduation was one of the proudest moments of my life. She went on to college, which also brought their own challenges, growth opportunities, and experiences. Although she has had her bumps along the way, Courtney found her footing. It is my greatest pleasure to witness her growth, into an amazingly strong, successful, intelligent, and compassionate young adult with a bright future ahead of her. She is looking forward toward graduate school with the goal of earning her Ph.D. in clinical psychology and I know that this path is her destiny, as my path was mine.

I am relieved that those terribly challenging middle and high school years are behind us, and filled with gratitude that she came through it all alive. Those years were an absolute nightmare, and could have ended in tragedy. Sadly, there are many thousands of kids and their parents who also suffer through their middle and high school years, unaware of what can help them survive or thrive. Courtney and I chose to share our most personal experiences with candor, in order to bust the pervasive wall of stigma and shame in order to educate and empower those who need it most. Because as we have come to believe, "we're all a little Krazy, it's what we do with our Krazy that counts!"

NOTE: COVID-19 has dramatically altered the entire scope of education across the primary, secondary, and higher education fields. Whereas prior to the Coronavirus, home and distance learning was virtually unheard of, now it is the norm. This opens up many new possibilities and also presents new challenges to consider that will inevitably change the face of how special needs services and assistance is provided. Stay tuned . . . we are in the midst of a massive change in the field of education—and our lives, unlike anything we could have ever imagined.

What We Have Learned and Things to Consider

There are many factors to take into account when it comes to appropriate or even optimal education for a child with special needs of any kind, including mental health. There are different levels of educational support and academic environments available. Understanding, identifying, and providing for these needs can be mind boggling, especially under stress. Here are some of the basic terms and concepts to understand as you navigate your way on the KrazyTrain of educating your KG.

—— Intervention and Referral Services (I & RS) Meeting ——

A parent or teacher can initiate an initial meeting with the school guidance department when a student is struggling in school. Based on the identified needs of the student, the next steps may include observation and/or educational testing to determine if a 504 plan or individualized education program (IEP) is appropriate. A parent may also obtain testing for their child on their own if they wish to gain a more timely or non-biased result and present the results to the school in order to start the process for services.

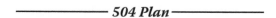

504 Plan

A legal document under section 504 of the Rehabilitation Act of 1973, a 504 plan provides for the needs of a child with a disability through classroom accommodations and can include extra time on tests and support services in school.

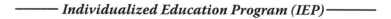

Individualized Education Program (IEP)

Also, a legal document to provide support for students with special needs, an individualized education program is a blueprint for services for children with disabilities. IEPs and 504 plans vary from state to state. Which one is better for the student depends on the nature of the child's disability and what they need to succeed in school.

Home Instruction

Home instruction is when the school district provides teachers and materials for a student to complete coursework at home. This can be accessed under approved circumstances, for a specific period (check with your district) if a specific medical or other condition does not allow a child to physically be in the classroom. This can be helpful for a short-term intervention to finish a marking period or a school year in progress if interrupted for medical reasons, including mental health. There are limits to what districts provide for a child approved for home instruction. Not all kinds of classes are always available (like labs or advanced placement classes), so check if this makes sense for your situation.

Homeschooling

There are many options and curriculum programs to support homeschooling, with more available all the time assisted by COVID-19. There are specific guidelines, including testing requirements and proficiency demonstrations. Homeschooling requires that parents be incredibly hands-on. This is certainly not right for everybody but can allow for freedom of choice and flexibility in many aspects of education that a traditional school usually cannot accommodate.

Out-of-District Placement

Out-of-district placement occurs when the home school cannot provide for the educational needs of a student within the district. This is usually a very expensive option, and most schools do not want to utilize out-of-district placements. More and more schools are becoming creative to provide for their students' needs within the district wherever possible.

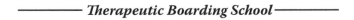

Therapeutic Boarding School

A therapeutic boarding school is an out-of-district placement that requires boarding due to its location. These schools can offer a plethora of potential therapeutic services along with a specialized academic curriculum and have a campus look and feel.

Residential Treatment School

When therapeutic treatment is the most important consideration, a residential treatment school is the most intensive option. These are essentially treatment programs with a school component. Quite restrictive, personal freedoms must be earned through a level system and intense supervision is present for the student. Oftentimes, a student goes through a wilderness program or is released from a hospital to a residential program when the student cannot maintain their safety in a less restrictive environment over a prolonged period.

These are the various types and levels of educational support available—from least intense to the most intense—and services and settings can level up or down as appropriate. A good rule of thumb is that the least intense, restrictive, or disruptive level that can meet a student's needs is usually best, although these decisions often have many moving parts and will vary based on the individual situation. Become educated, trust your gut, and advocate as necessary.

EXPERT ADVICE

Ashley DiBiasi, Psy.D, is a school psychologist at Lakeland Regional High School, where Courtney enrolled as a junior. She was Courtney's key point of contact in every way during her junior and senior years, from in-school therapist to academic advisor, to tough love boundary keeper for us all during those difficult times. Courtney and I went back to see Ashley when Courtney was a sophomore in college to interview her for this book. It was a wonderful experience to sit with Ashley after all Courtney had been through in high school— there were smiles and warm hugs and it was remarkable to share that moment together. Here is what Ashley had to say about success in school when there are mental health considerations at play.

What is important for young people and their parents to understand about dealing with school while struggling with mental or emotional health issues?

If possible, it is so important to keep up with your academic schoolwork. The more a student falls behind on their assignments, the more stress and anxiety will build up. This leads to panic, and sometimes paralysis where students are so overwhelmed, they stop doing anything. School avoidance can unfortunately follow. If needed, ask teachers for support. Extended deadlines may be helpful, but it is important to not become over reliant upon them.

What support services may be available to help young people who are struggling in school?

All students have access to a school (guidance) counselor. A counselor is assigned to each student in every school. These counselors provide academic and social/emotional support. There are also school psychologists and school social workers in most schools. These professionals work with special education students, and depending on the district, general education students too.

How do people go about obtaining these support services?

If a student has a medical diagnosis, mental health diagnoses included, they could be eligible for a 504 plan if their symptoms severely limit their ability to learn in school. This could provide some accommodations throughout the day, such as extra time, preferential seating, and the ability to seek out a nurse or counselor when needed. If a student has a mental health diagnosis and it is significantly impacting the student enough to where they require special education and related services, they can be evaluated to see if they are eligible for an IEP. An IEP can provide accommodations and modifications to the curriculum, meaning teaching and assignments can be altered for a student to access them more easily. When appropriate, students with mental health diagnoses can be enrolled in special programs or out of district schools; however, these are serious decisions as they can significantly restrict a student's right to be educated with their general education peers.

What else is important to understand about academic concerns and options?

As said before, it is so important to keep up with assignments. It may be difficult for students with high personal standards, but they need to turn things in even if the product is not perfect. I often see high achieving students become paralyzed and unwilling to move forward on an essay, for example, because they know they are not in a place to create something up to their standards. It is important to just start writing—begin with an outline to guide you and keep you organized as your thoughts are often all over the place when managing mental health issues. Fill in the outline and begin writing. Be OK with turning in the minimum if it keeps you from getting a zero. It may sound like odd advice but lowering your academic standards in a time of crisis will help you to accomplish more than if you are only willing to turn in stellar work. Please take advantage of any support that is out there. In addition to parents, siblings, and friends, your school offers opportunities to receive help. This is essential as outside therapy is not always feasible for some.

Another interesting perspective from inside a traditional high school comes from **Mary Cunningham, LPC,** who is the student assistance coordinator for the Caldwell-West Caldwell School District in West Caldwell, New Jersey, (which coincidentally is the same high school that I graduated from, but that was *way* before her time there). Warm and engaging, Mary is a supportive advocate for students struggling with any issue whether emotional, physical, or academic. I have worked with Mary for many years as a collaborative therapist in the community, providing therapy to some of the students that Mary assists at school. It is impressive to witness how Mary consistently goes above and beyond to get her students what they need to succeed.

What are some of the things parents of struggling teens should know about obtaining support services in school?

Parents are understandably protective about sharing private information with schools, especially mental health and emotional challenges. Yet, kids spend more time in school than anywhere else. Therefore, it is important to develop relationships that are supportive at school. Most people go into education because they care about the whole child (not just the academic child), but they can't really respond and help if they do not know what is going on behind the scenes. I encourage parents and students to reach out to someone at school they feel they can trust. This can be a nurse, student assistance counselor, guidance counselor, or even a trusted teacher.

Some parents are concerned about how private information will be noted in a student's file and how this information may be disclosed in the future with colleges. Student confidentiality exists and is protected by law, so ask about your schools' policies if you are concerned about this. School-based services, once identified, are often optional, not mandatory. Exploring what may be helpful does not mean those options will be put into place without your agreement. Depending upon the school, these may include support like small groups on topics such as coping with social issues, anxiety or grief, or school-based counseling.

Can you discuss some of the social concerns students may be dealing with?

Today's social media and gaming culture make it really hard to step back and unplug. It exists 24/7 and creates emotional and social consequences that are hard to perceive. Teachers and parents may not have access to this virtual world. It is important to understand the pressure that this creates on kids, because they are saturated all the time. As a counselor, I always ask about students' screen-time 'diet' and try to educate them about their consumption much the same way that we talk about food: what's healthy, what's junk food, what's a normal portion size and what tends to make you break out in hives? Feelings and mood are impacted both by how we experience real-time and virtual time. Creating opportunities to unplug are strongly encouraged. School-based activities can help build real relationships, skills, and confidence. This can be through clubs, theater, sports or anything where the emphasis is on a shared experience or building a skill, rather than focusing on social status.

Here, I must add a note about COVID-19 and the devastation it has wreaked upon every aspect of the lives of students, families, and educators. Nothing is the same at all in any way. It is ironic—a new phenomenon I see in what is now my one hundred percent virtual therapy practice is the struggle to do school virtually, or with masks on. A and B days, virtual learning, the yearning for human face-to-face contact has never been more complicated or elusive!

While Ashley and Mary's advice is helpful for students able to remain in their home school district, sometimes a student may need to receive their education in a different environment. This can be a very confusing and highly emotional process. There are various options for education outside the home school district, including religious and secular day schools, traditional boarding schools, therapeutic boarding schools, and residential treatment facilities. I see this issue play out within my practice, and I can certainly relate to parents who wonder if there is a better place for their struggling child to grow and thrive. We may wonder if a different school could help get to the root cause of the challenges our child is facing, or if we can afford it. These are heart wrenching, important questions that deserve consideration, and enlisting the support of a professional who can help figure this out can be very helpful.

——————— *Educational Consultants and* ———————
Treatment Placement Consultants

Educational consultants and treatment placement specialists are professionals who can help sort through the multitude of options appropriate for individual circumstances. Usually, an educational consultant is hired by the family for a fee to do significant leg work necessary to place a student outside of the home school. A treatment placement specialist usually works directly for a company that owns and operates different treatment facilities. There is usually no fee for the treatment specialist's services, but placement recommendations will come from within the network of affiliated facilities they represent. Consulting with a specialist about educational or treatment options is worthy of consideration, because educational placement is a big-ticket item with high stakes.

Lucy Pritzker of Elm Street Placements, which has offices in Manhattan and New Jersey, provides educational and therapeutic consulting services to families worldwide. She has recently authored a book that is a parent's guide to residential placement for struggling teens. Lucy helps parents find the most appropriate mental health treatment available for their child. Sometimes there is an academic component involved, but not always.

What is an educational consultant?

The more accurate name for what I do is really therapeutic placement specialist. I figure out what will be most helpful for an individual child and their family. This is a whole new world that families are thrust into, often during the worst crisis of their lives. I advise the family exactly what will be most beneficial for their children, keeping only their best interests in mind. We have visited each of the programs we recommend, we know the individual therapists, the student body, and the issues they treat best. Our job is to get to know the student and all of the complex factors involved and match them with the very best possible program to meet their needs. We also stick close with our families every step of the way, to provide much needed support and guidance throughout the entire process.

When may the time be right for a family to consider placing their child?

Parents may consider the following factors while taking into account that every situation is different:

- *If things have escalated to the point that a child is not safe at home anymore and a short stabilization will not suffice.*
- *If a child asks to go, this should be considered, and options should be explored.*
- *The family is suffering so greatly that siblings or other family members are impacted.*
- *The tolerance for remaining in the home has been reached, for example drug use has not stopped, or too much school has been missed.*
- *A child's social, emotional, intellectual, or academic needs are not being met and a more well-suited environment would be better for them. This does not need to involve medication, therapy, or restrictions.*

Can you please discuss some financial considerations?

Most programs I work with are private pay. Insurance may cover a certain portion, but this is not a guarantee. If there is an IEP in place, the school district may pay a portion, but that is case and state specific, and not always easy to obtain. This is where an educational advocate or attorney may be helpful to consider utilizing.

Lauren Milner, MSW, is a senior treatment placement specialist who works directly with a large treatment corporation. Lauren is a very special person with tremendous placement expertise who is very close to my heart. We have worked together for many years.

What is a treatment placement specialist?

I help people find appropriate treatment. Many times, a therapist or doctor will reach out to me to assist them in placing their person who needs a higher level of care. I speak to the individual and their family to gather all of the necessary information, including financial and insurance information to make the most appropriate referral possible. I also support them through all phases of treatment, from the initial referral through discharge. I am there one hundred percent every step of the way. Treatment placement specialists help families through some of the most difficult times they will ever face, and the expertise and support they can provide is invaluable.

Here are some questions you may want to ask when considering a therapeutic or residential program:

- What is the program treatment philosophy and how long has it been in operation?
- How many therapy sessions are included weekly, and what type (group, individual, family)? Are there specialty therapies such as yoga, body therapies, etc?
- Is there an individual clinician and family therapist consistent throughout treatment?
- How is school incorporated into the program? What kind of academic support exists? Is there a college prep component, or honors or AP classes? What colleges have their graduates attended?

- What is available to do during non-therapy or non-school time?
- What kind of family involvement is there? Do families come in for training/ therapy?
- Where is the nearest medical facility? How are medical situations managed?
- What are the financial obligations? Is there a clearly spelled out policy?
- What is the average length of stay? How is this determined?
- How is aftercare and discharge planning handled?

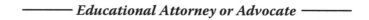

Educational Attorney or Advocate

There may come a time when the services of an educational attorney or an advocate may become necessary, usually when what a parent believes is necessary for their child significantly differs from what the school district is offering.

Paul Barger, Esquire, of Barger and Gaines, located in Irvington, New York is a top-notch educational attorney who is extremely knowledgeable and compassionate. Here is what Paul had to say about the thorny and confusing topic of special needs and school from a legal perspective.

What, exactly, is an educational attorney? Why would somebody want to use their services? How is this different from an educational advocate?

A special education attorney provides a variety of services to families. In some matters, our primary role is to advocate for additional services for a student, or for a change in program, or to take steps to ensure the district is properly implementing the IEP. In other cases, known as 'unilateral placement' cases, we focus on seeking reimbursement for the costs incurred by families relating to private school placements. There are certain cases where our involvement is simply to assist in facilitating the relationship between a family and a district. The primary difference between a special education attorney and a special education advocate is the due process hearing. While there are advocates who represent families at hearings, when a case goes to litigation, such as in a unilateral placement case, most families opt for representation by an attorney. There can, however, be overlap in the efforts of special education attorneys and special education advocates, and our firm employs a hybrid model of legal representation and advocacy because of the different needs of each family and each student.

We always conduct a thorough review of each student's records, we assess the case, and we confer with educational professionals to learn about a child's needs. We also refer families to educational professionals so the child can be evaluated and so the family has a better sense of what a child requires in order to receive an appropriate educational program.

It is not easy to navigate the public education process, and that is especially true if there is a breakdown in the relationship between the family and the district. Special education attorneys can, and should, serve as the point person to assist families in getting the information they need and then securing appropriate programs and services."

What are some of the most important things a parent or a young person should know about what is reasonable for a school to provide to struggling children and teenagers?

Every case and every situation require an analysis of the learning profile of the individual student. Two students with the same disabling condition may be struggling in school in different ways. It is essential to look at the student's disability, determine how it is impacting the student, and then develop a program individualized to address that student's needs.

I often hear from families that a district did not find a child eligible for special education and related services because, according to the district, the student 'just has anxiety.' That is an incomplete analysis. In that situation, there is a diagnosed disability, and the district must then ask whether the disability is having an impact on the student's education. The district must determine whether the impact is such that the child requires special education and related services.

The key to the analysis is the impact on the student in school. It is also important to note that 'education' is not synonymous with 'academics.' While education, of course, includes academics, it also encompasses a student's social, emotional, and behavioral needs. Dismissing a student's needs because the student 'just has anxiety' does not consider the impact of the student's anxiety on his/her performance in school.

Districts are charged with providing a multitude of programs and services to students with IEPs, depending upon the individual needs of each student. Families are often unaware that districts not only need to offer instruction by certified special education teachers, but also programs and services such as social skills, counseling, executive functioning training, speech/language therapy, occupational therapy, and physical therapy. And that is not an exhaustive list. There are numerous programs and services available to students with special needs, and it is incumbent upon districts to inform families of options, and to identify the types of support a particular student may require.

In addition, students eligible for IEPs are entitled to testing accommodations and classroom modifications to allow students to access the curriculum.

Common accommodations/modifications include, but are not limited to, extra time on tests, extra time on assignments, preferential seating, study guides, note-taking assistance, assistive technology, and many other reasonable supports designed to level the playing field for students with special needs. Students not found eligible for special education and related services, but who have a diagnosed disability and who require accommodations/ modifications, may receive those accommodations/ modifications through a Section 504 Plan.

Is there anything else you think would be helpful for people to understand about your services?

No two cases are ever the same. We approach each case based upon the family's goals and based upon the input of educational professionals. It may be the matter will involve a unilateral placement in a private school and a dispute with the district over reimbursement, but it may also be that our efforts are to improve the student's individual program in the district.

We encourage all families to review the parental rights guide, which each district is required to provide. Those guides do not provide all the information parents need, but it is very important for parents to be aware of the rights of their children. We also encourage families to address educational concerns as early as possible. If there is a concern, request an evaluation, or seek the input of private educational professionals. Gather as much information as possible, and advocate from preschool through graduation or age twenty-one.

Any last words of wisdom you wish to share?

The families that meet with the most success with their districts are those who are prepared and knowledgeable. Parents can accomplish a great deal for their children when they have the information about the child's needs and about the special education process. And, when possible, let the students have a say in his/her education. Students should have a seat at the IEP table, as they are often their own best advocates.

What About College?

For many young people and their families, college is a major consideration throughout the high school years. As parents, we want our children to receive the very best education possible, not only for the sake of that education, but also to set them up for their best options for college and their future. For KGs, there are legitimate concerns about the high school experience, and what can make the most sense regarding college. Some parents worry that the stigma of a mental health challenge might limit their child's chances of admission at certain schools. They also may struggle to determine if mental health should be discussed in the application. Another concern can be the ability to ensure that college support services will be adequately available. Certain colleges are much better than others when it comes to providing students with academic or other support services on campus, leading most experts to agree that due diligence is important when choosing a college.

Another consideration for college involves counseling services. Will KG continue with their home therapist and medical professionals? If so, how frequently? Does a new therapist or doctor need to be set up in advance on or near campus? What about the availability of group therapy such as Dialectical Behavior Therapy (DBT) on campus? It is also important to consider how to handle a psychiatric emergency in advance. I have heard horror stories of poorly handled psych emergencies turning into traumatic nightmares. More than one student I know personally has been hospitalized for sharing concerning information with an ill-informed school counselor who did not understand the history of that student. I love the old adage here, "Hope for the best, but prepare for the worst." It is more helpful to plan if possible than clean up a mess after the fact.

Dr. David Nast, PhD, is the Director of the Office of Specialized Services at Ramapo College of New Jersey. Dr. Nast is a kind and gentle man, who is clearly enthusiastic about sharing his take on success strategies for college. Courtney says that all her friends who know David love him!

What are your suggestions for college students with disabilities of any kind?

Affiliate with your college disabilities office as soon as possible, before classes start. Some students think that they will wait and see how things go, thinking that they will get a fresh start in college. It is better to be connected from the very beginning. For most students, the first semester of college is the hardest, and any disabilities office will have a process of affiliation that will take time. So having services and relationships in place, rather than trying to obtain them in a crisis, is the best way to go. College is a very different environment than high school and there is much less stigma in college. You are still doing all the work and achieving your own success. The services are for support, they do not do the work for you.

What advice do you have for parents?

Make yourself aware of what services are available on campus in order to guide your student towards what can be most helpful and appropriate for them. For example, 'Have you reached out to the writing or counseling center?' Disabilities offices expect parents to be involved in the beginning, but as students mature and progress in their college experience, they will take on more self-direction.

Any other words of wisdom you can share?

Those students that affiliate with disabilities services have college graduation rates equal to or even greater than students in the general population. Use the services that are available to assist you as you achieve your hard-earned success in college and beyond.

To gain an understanding of what accommodations and services might look like in college, consider the following:

Eligible disabilities usually include but are not limited to:

- Attention Deficit Disorder
- Blindness or Visual Impairments
- Cerebral Palsy
- Chronic Illnesses (AIDS, Arthritis, Cancer, Cardiac

Disease, Diabetes, Etc.)
- Deafness or Hearing Impairments
- Epilepsy or Seizure Disorders
- Learning Disabilities
- Psychiatric Disabilities of all kinds including Anxiety, Depression, etc.
- Orthopedic Impairments
- Speech Disorders
- Traumatic Brain Injury

Services and accommodations that may be available might include, but are not limited to:

- Textbooks in Alternate Format
- Notetakers
- Readers
- Scribes
- Testing Accommodations
- Use of Adaptive Equipment
- Academic Counseling (Time Management, Organization, and Study Skills, Etc.)
- Advocacy and Liaison with Faculty/Staff
- Assistance with Course Selection/Registration
- Self-Advocacy Training
- Refer for Career Counseling
- Refer for Peer Tutoring
- Refer for Personal Counseling, and Campus or Community Services

The above is a good overview of what might be available for college support or accommodations. Most colleges and universities will have some or most of these services but be sure to ask them directly. I recommend that you visit the counseling center or disabilities office when on a college tour. Check if they are located in a basement or in some far off part of campus, and take the time to discuss their approach to student services. Setting up services in advance is key, especially with counseling. There can be problems with availability, especially a few weeks after the semester begins, so do not wait until services are needed to obtain them. I can't tell you how many disabilities forms I have filled out as a therapist for my patients over the years, too often when they come back home brokenhearted after a failed semester. I have also witnessed significant variance in the quality of support services from school to school. As with all things in KrazyLand, do your research in advance and be prepared to help your KG be a good advocate for themself. Lastly, the best accommodation of all in my opinion is a designated point of contact who meets with students on a regular basis. This way, someone on the inside knows the student over time and can help them access whatever services make the most sense for their situation.

Routine legal paperwork

When kids turn eighteen, they become legal adults. Therefore, having proper medical and other release forms in place *in advance,* prior to them leaving for school, is necessary in order to assist them with proper access whenever needed. These forms can vary from state to state so be sure to ask the college what they suggest having in place so you are covered. These forms might include:

- **Health Insurance Portability and Accountability ACT (HIPAA) forms.** This is a privacy release to discuss confidentiality protected matters.

- **Medical Power of Attorney.** This names an authorized agent for medical decisions if necessary.

- **General durable power of attorney**. This person makes financial transactions and legal decisions.

- **Family Educational Rights and Privacy Act (FERPA) form**. This allows you speak to the school and/or access grades and other academic matters.

MARCI

Upon reflecting on this chapter, I am struck by the high level of importance education holds within my family of origin. I come from a long line of highly educated women going back to my grandmother, Mollie, who was a college-educated professional woman in the 1950s when it was highly unusual. My mother and sisters all have advanced degrees, frequently more than one. As much as I was a Level Three KrazyGirl, I still earned my master's degree and professional licenses. It was assumed that Courtney, her sister, and all her maternal cousins would attend the best colleges they could gain access to.

When my children were younger, I had preconceived notions about what a "good college" meant and spent a considerable amount of time thinking about and discussing this subject. When Courtney's package of Krazy was delivered and her life's path derailed, I had no choice but to completely rethink what her college education might involve. Before, it was all about "the college experience" and college rankings. Afterwards it morphed into things like proximity to home and meaningful support services. Ultimately, even with all our planning, Courtney still transferred colleges halfway through her first semester freshman year. She finally found her place at the same small school in the woods where I'd found my own fantastic college thirty-five years earlier. The irony is not lost on me. I think the lesson in all of this for me, is that we can work hard to pave a good path but we can't know how things will ultimately play out, so we are well served to check our preconceived notions at the door. I now see that that I was a school snob and have come to view educational success measured by an entirely different set of metrics.

Krazy really does play out on a school stage. The complex interplay between the ever-changing adolescent brain and academics, social life, relationships, self-esteem, growing independence, and mental health issues is extremely complicated. Success in one area can branch out and build success in other areas; however, when one part of the developing self is negatively affected, this, too, will expand. Parents need to stay involved whenever possible to guide this process, while also providing for KG's increasing need for autonomy and self-expression. This is a delicate balancing act with targets that are constantly shifting. As always, paying close attention to your values and intuition will guide you. As young people begin to increasingly take on the lead role in the production of their own lives, parents will direct more from backstage and eventually come to sit in the audience. This natural process will ebb and flow as time passes, and one day an entirely new scene will set the stage for the next comedy or tragedy that is our life.

CHAPTER 6

Relationships:
We All Need to Belong

"Well, we all need someone we can lean on,
and if you want it, you can lean on me."
—The Rolling Stones

"All and all you're just another brick in the wall . . . "
—Pink Floyd

MARCI

We come into our very being through human connection and are destined to live our lives within the context of relationships. We are programmed, both hard-wired and soft-loaded, to crave, need, and require human interaction. Nothing can bring us greater joy or cause us deeper pain than our most important personal relationships. The safety and pleasure we share with each other is necessary for both wellbeing and the survival of our species. We also know what devastating results the deprivation of human contact can bring about; the torture that isolation wreaks on the body and soul is undeniable. Indeed, human relationships are the ever-shifting bedrock and the lifeblood we all share.

Good and satisfying relationships are not easy to achieve or sustain. We are drawn toward and repelled from each other with magnetic force. Like the famous saying goes, "We can't live with them, and we can't live without them!" (Well, that quote refers to women, but you get it . . .) It has taken me close to *six decades* of life to feel like I have finally come to peace with much of my relationship Krazy, although some of my family members may disagree. I think this is because it has taken me a long time to finally feel comfortable in my own skin. If I don't feel good inside myself, I can't be good with others. My inner *ish* bleeds out onto the playing field with everyone I encounter, be this my family of origin, family of creation, friends, coworkers, lovers, or the world at large.

For too many years of my life, this has been the case. Not that things are perfect now, but I have achieved a higher level of relational success through the hard work I have put into this worthy quest. My conditioned defensive responses[5] are less automatic now, so I take time to respond according to my values, and not just react to stress. I finally understand that cleaning up relationship messes is harder to do than preventing them in the first place. I credit my hardest times and deepest struggles to this personal growth and development, and also to a little help from my friends and the benevolent force of grace.

When I was young and in the midst of my Level Three Batshit KrazyDays, what was most painful for me was feeling alone. I did not feel connected to my family, I didn't feel like I fit in at school, and I had no activities where I belonged. I judged and hated myself in complete isolation. My response to this pain was rage and despair. I ran away from home and lived in squalid conditions with people I would never have allowed my own kids to spend time with. My

---

5   Patterns of emotional response, developed during earlier life experiences. See the Family Dynamics chapter for an expanded exploration of this concept.

parents were in a state of shock and confusion about these choices—why would a kid from a good family and a nice neighborhood live with bikers? (Why would Patty Hurst leave the family compound and run off with the Symbionese Liberation Army?) The reason for me was simple: I felt like I belonged there and they accepted me. I felt like I had a badass gang behind me that always had my back, because, in fact, they did. I am blessed to still have some of my best and most loyal lifetime friends from back in those insane days. Many of those relationships would go on to become the bedrock of my life's journey forward. In numerous ways, I credit the trust, intimacy, and nurturance of those misfit relationships for the wonderful life that I enjoy today.

Looking back, I can see why I made many of the relationship choices I did. My self-esteem was completely non-existent. I was both grandiose and full of shame. I had no boundaries and, at the same time, was totally walled off from others. In RLT[6] terminology, I was as far away from 'the center of health' as a person could be. I felt either "better than" or "worse than" other people. It is always lonely on either side of that equation. I now understand that this divide we experience is largely based on the judgements and shame we secretly hold. For humans to feel connected with others, we need to be a person among people, no better or worse than others. This requires that we let go of conscious and unconscious judgements, many of which we unwittingly inherited as our family dynamics rolled downhill. This is not an easy task. Relational health, be it with our parents, kids, spouses, or the person bagging our groceries, depends on a world view that simultaneously values ourselves and others. Imagine the Buddha comfortably seated, softly smiling, with arms extended and fists closed. In each hand there contains a sacred scroll of paper. On one it reads, "I am a divine child of God—perfect

---

6   RLT or Relational Life Therapy, created by Terry Real. Information can be found about this relationship and therapy model in the chapter on Therapy, under Family Therapy.

as I am." On the other it reads, "I am but a speck of dust that exists in a vast and mysterious universe." Healthy relationships with other human beings require that we embody a bit of both.

There are some basic elements involved in creating and maintaining healthy and satisfying relationships. One of the most important is learning to trust and verify our feelings and intuition. Paying attention to our values is a key part of this. When we build confidence, we can see others with more clarity, and can intentionally choose where they should fit in our lives. Managing expectations in relationships is also critical, reducing frustration and friction. Interpersonal effectiveness skills can be cultivated, which helps us respond rather than react when challenges arise. The ability to work through problems in relationships is necessary, so becoming comfortable with communication and conflict resolution is critical. Building comfort with boundaries helps all our relationships, but especially so when romantic feelings arise, and things get even more complicated. All these elements require thoughtful effort, but the results are well worth it. Positive connections with others are some of the greatest gifts life has to offer us. Let's look at each of these elements in greater detail.

Trust, But Verify

Ronald Reagan is famously quoted in his high stakes negotiations during the Cold War nuclear disarmament process saying, "trust but verify." Trust is a huge part of any good relationship, but verification is also important. This begins with knowing and trusting ourselves. When we listen to our inner guidance system about what is right for us, we can maneuver appropriately. For example, I hate gossip. I don't want to be around it and prefer to not engage with those who do. If I am on the soccer field, or out with other moms, and I notice that people are beginning to gossip, I can feel myself tensing up and distancing. This is my body giving signals to pay attention to my intuition, which helps me navigate the situation. Other times, I might feel drawn toward or interested in somebody. This feeling moves me to want to spend more time with them or develop that relationship. Our gut feelings help guide us to move closer to or away from others, which informs the choices we make in social situations or in our relationships. Trusting our intuition is a key factor, but we must also verify the information we get, through observation and experience over time. When we trust ourselves, verify information, and respond in ways that align with our values, we can navigate our relationships with greater confidence.

Trusting others builds upon the foundation of trusting ourselves. This process takes time to develop and can also be broken in an instant. Feeling safe and secure in relationships grows over time, usually through shared experiences, which can be both positive and challenging. Loyalty is also an important part of trust and creates a bedrock of safety in our closest relationships. There is nothing quite like having a true friend who really has your back, through thick and thin. However, this needs to be a two-way street. We must also be loyal and trustworthy to receive this in return. Sometimes, trust in relationships requires the ability to admit when we have made a mistake. No one is perfect. When we own up and can work through the things we have done to create a rupture in a relationship, this builds trust and shows we can be accountable for our actions. This also shows a higher level of self-awareness and compassion for the feelings of others. Relationships thrive in an environment of trust, but this must be verified over time. When we cherish our most important relationships as the rare and valuable gifts that they are, they will nurture us in return. To have a good friend, we must be a good friend.

Popularity and Values

Popularity is a slippery slope and not always a true metric of self-worth. Without a solid set of personal values, it can be easy to lose yourself to the desire to be liked by others. There are two types of popularity. The first comes when individuals are genuinely liked or admired, so many people wish to connect with them. The second is based largely on anxiety, fear, or the potential for personal gain. Let's dig a little deeper here. There are those individuals people seek out because they have desirable personal qualities, traits, or something positive to offer; therefore, many hold them in high regard. These people are liked, desired, or admired for who they are, or what they bring to others. Other types of popularity are based on gaining social status or exclusivity, much like the movie *Mean Girls*. This cohort can propel others to a higher status, or alternatively, reduce standing to rubble, at will. The more influence is wielded, the more powerful, elusive, or unattainable access becomes. Like a Birkin bag, the harder it is to get, the more both the price and desirability increases. Gaining popularity can be a ticket to approval, acceptance, or a validation of self-worth. Other times, popularity involves leveraging connections for opportunities that would otherwise be unavailable. It is human nature to want to surround ourselves, through others, with what we desire the most. It's important to carefully consider what really motivates us in order to successfully navigate the minefields of popularity. The more we are in touch with what really matters, the more we can represent this in the choices we make with our relationships.

The acceptance that popularity implies can be a tempting, yet risky, attraction. Getting caught up in a popularity race can be an easy way to lose yourself. It can be very difficult for KGs who are young, vulnerable, or desperately want love and acceptance to understand the complications of social and emotional relationships. Our hearts break when we or our loved ones are excluded, feel lonely, or choose the wrong people over and over again. Issues of fake friends, popularity, or social status are challenging to make sense of, regardless of our age. This is why it is so important to do our relational work[7] as soon as possible in life. We are never too young or too old to do this work. Learning about our emotional triggers, understanding where they originate from, staying connected to our values, and remaining mindful

7   Investigation of patterns developed in our early lives, that tend to replay again and again with others, unless understood and reworked.

of our goals sets the emotional tone in all our relationships. Nothing good happens when we are swept up in the riptide of our emotions and react, rather than respond to relationship challenges. We find our true people and feel the most comfortable with others when we stay connected to our core values.

Managing Expectations: Our Inner Circle

Understanding what we can expect from others is essential in good relationships. We can't get water out of an empty well, so to speak. The ability to *discern*, or see what people are really about, is an important relationship skill. As we have discussed, if we observe the behavior of others, we can usually see how we want them to fit in our lives and make necessary adjustments along the way. Doing this without taking things personally, or getting into negative self-talk, is the best approach. This may sound calculating, and to some degree, it is. Deciding how to best respond to others, regardless of how we are connected to them, is important for our comfort and safety. Whether they are family members, friends, coworkers, or acquaintances, we get to decide how we wish to relate to them. This is especially true in changing political climates, or in the age of COVID-19, or any other larger challenges, where our values and comfort zone may differ tremendously from that of others.

Our relationships hold great influence over our thoughts, feelings, behaviors, health, and wellbeing. The intentional placement of a person on the chess board of our lives, whether in our inner or outer circle, makes all the difference in how we feel. We have the ability to move people closer to us or farther away as makes sense. We can even kick someone off our board if we find they are toxic or harmful to us. It is our prerogative and responsibility to decide.

Here is a personal example. I have a friend I used to consider part of my inner circle. However, we could not talk out conflict and when I would try, she would ghost me for weeks. This was really upsetting, and I began to make up stories in my head about why this was happening. I concluded that I must not mean that much to her, which was confusing. If we were so close, why couldn't we talk through our emotions with each other? When I finally stepped back and saw things more clearly, I realized that she was conflict avoidant with *everybody* in her life. This trait played out with other friends, her kids, and even her husband. She was clearly not comfortable dealing with conflict, and that had nothing to do with *me*. Based on this new understanding, I adjusted my expectations and no longer looked for that deeper connection with her. Now, I don't become frustrated, and I can appreciate the relationship for the many positive aspects it has. I didn't want to kick her off my chessboard, I just moved her back a few squares by adjusting my expectations. Consider this dynamic and how it collides with my own unfinished relationship business, and it is clear how complicated our human interactions can be.

Not all people will become a part of or stay in our inner circle forever. In order to be comfortable in our relationships, we need to see them with clarity, try to see ourselves with clarity, keep others in the correct placement, and manage our expectations appropriately. There may also be the rare and unexpected gift of a person, who appears out of nowhere, and becomes a dear and lifelong friend. The ability to be also open-minded and flexible helps us put people in the right spot for us, relate to them accordingly and adjust accordingly over time.

We Can Work It Out

There are times when we run into problems with the people in our lives. When this happens, we need to be able to manage conflict and communicate effectively in order to restore balance. It is unrealistic to expect that just because we care about or are connected to someone, we will get along with them all the time. When we talk our issues out, we can get to the other side of misunderstandings quickly and effectively. We might even find that we come to feel the closest to those we can work things out with. Conversely, the inability to work through challenges may be the deal breaker that ends a relationship.

The first thing to keep in mind is that conflict in relationships is normal. No two people will ever see eye to eye on every subject, all the time. Working through these difficulties can be challenging, but there are things we can do that make it easier to deal with. When a disagreement happens, it is important to remain calm, and try to stay open minded. If the problem is small or an unusual circumstance, things may work themselves out with a little patience and understanding. However, avoiding an ongoing situation creates an elephant in the room that needs to be danced around. That is not a sustainable strategy over the long haul. As I shared in the example above with my conflict avoidant friend, not dealing with issues that arise will eventually compromise, reduce, or end most relationships. However, the shift in perspective may also need to come from us.

Communication is a two-way street. Each person needs to be able to share their perspective, and also hear the other person out. Focusing on the issue at hand, with an open heart, increases understanding and moves toward resolution. On the other hand, blame or accusations will undermine good will, and block the give and take process necessary to resolve the problem. We might feel justified in becoming defensive or refusing to see where the other person is coming from, but that will not move things forward. We may need to accept that a different viewpoint is not necessarily wrong. When we can open up and explore challenges with respect and empathy, we can move forward and put most issues behind us. The ability to work things out with others is often the main factor separating an acquaintance from a true friend.

Interpersonal Effectiveness

The joy and satisfaction that comes from healthy connections with others is profound and life altering. The more we cultivate positive relationships, the more comfortable and enjoyable we'll find the overall quality of our lives. For most people, but especially for KGs, the area of interpersonal effectiveness can be elusive, confusing, or downright mystifying! Building meaningful relationships with others takes dedicated focus and intentional energy, which involves skills that can be learned if they do not come naturally.

Dialectical Behavioral Therapy[8] has an entire module devoted to the important topic of interpersonal effectiveness. This concept is also referred to as *emotional intelligence* (EQ), which involves the effective use of healthy relationship skills. Social literacy, which is the ability to read, understand, and effectively manage emotions and conflict in relationships, is crucial for relational success. Most KGs have some degree of difficulty with this. As Courtney shares in her section in this chapter, mental health issues can make it even more difficult to show up well for our relationships. There is often the challenge of our own inner critic, who can mercilessly pass judgment or create internal shame.

Relationships are difficult enough to navigate without the complications of anxiety, depression, autism, etc. Fortunately, even if interpersonal effectiveness skills do not come naturally, they can be learned and improved upon when practiced over time. There are many wonderful resources that teach interpersonal effectiveness skills in detail, and there are some great ones listed in the recommended reading section at the back of this book. There are also various training modules available online, so please take some time to investigate this subject, if applicable.

Boundaries: Protective, Containing, Rigid, and Open

Boundaries are an essential element in healthy relationships. My favorite definition of boundaries comes from the amazing Brene Brown. In her work, *Rising Strong* (2015), she succinctly explains boundaries as "simply our lists of what's OK and what's not OK."

---

8   DBT: Dialectical Behavioral Therapy: created by Marsha Linehan, see the chapter on Therapy for further explanation.

All family and relationship experts emphasize the need for healthy personal boundaries in relationships. There are two basic forms of boundaries. **Protective boundaries** are the walls we put up to keep ourselves safe, like physical space or passwording our personal emails or media. **Containing boundaries** keep our bad stuff in, such as an intense anger flare up, oversharing, or learning to watch our words to avoid hurting someone's feelings. Both types of boundaries are necessary and important for healthy relationships with others. Boundary lines can sometimes become blurred, especially if the family we came from had poor boundaries and we did not learn along the way. Boundaries can be overly **rigid** and unyielding, or too open and porous. If we are overly rigid, we try to control others or need to have things go our way. If we are too **open**, we can become swayed by others, from our truth or direction. There is a tremendous amount of information to be considered in this important topic, and I encourage a deeper dive into this.

More Than Friends

In this chapter, we have taken a close look at many of the aspects that make up healthy and satisfying interpersonal relationships. The importance of trust and verification, staying true to our values, and becoming empowered to make good relationship choices cannot be emphasized enough. Then, oftentimes when we least expect it, comes a powerful complication: the element of sexual and romantic feelings.

There is nothing quite like the powerful human emotions of attraction. The undeniable experience of magic, kismet, desire, or lust can knock us off our feet. Regardless of the object of our romantic interest, when those feelings come to call, the sensation can be overwhelming. Romantic connections are the stuff of romance novels and hit singles. At the same time, this section of the pool is fraught with challenges that can be as intense as the feelings themselves. It is all too easy to push aside our logic or reason when we find ourselves in the deep end. Take a deep breath. All will be well. We can enjoy the magic that comes with "more than friends," if we follow a few simple guidelines.

The same principles of healthy relationships apply to *all types* of relationships. That's right. As much as we might want to ignore these guidelines when it comes to an uber hot prospect, this is not advisable. Even if we think we are just fooling around, too often we fall in love. The more we desire another person, the less we want anything to get in the way of the possibilities that might happen. All too frequently, passion clouds sound judgement. Many people, especially when younger, are particularly susceptible to becoming deeply attached once physicality occurs, even if that is not the original intention. When we allow others into our most intimate physical spaces, we are actually letting them into the deepest parts of our souls.

To avoid the common pitfalls the element of romance can create, the best strategy is to stay connected to our core values. This means that especially in the early stages of a new romantic relationship, we must trust less and verify more. Maintain healthy personal boundaries, so you have the time to really see who this beautiful new person actually is. Do their values and interests dovetail well with your own? How do they relate to their family, their finances, their health, or the waiter who serves you in the restaurant? Are you comfortable with what you see beyond the surface? Are you actually compatible with this lovely new prospect? Being discerning in the early stages of a new romantic relationship can help avoid the pain of loss later on. Manage your expectations with clarity and a mature perspective. By all means, have fun and enjoy the exciting energy that can only come with chemistry, but also try to keep your head on straight with your feet firmly on the ground. The emotions of the heart can obscure the clarity of the mind like nothing else.

You have ceased to lay hold of my heart that I sold,
for passion that surely was masked—

by a merry go round of pain lost and then found,
reliving our childhood pasts.

We found in each other, one thing and another,
but one thing I know now for sure—

is that previous pain cannot be reclaimed,
and passion cannot be the cure.

Too long have I struggled, for years I have juggled,
the lessons a young woman learns.

And now I can see, it was all meant to be . . .

But for you now, I no longer yearn."

—Marci Wolff, 1988, Pacific Coast Highway, somewhere north of
Los Angeles, California

COURTNEY

Relationships are everywhere. From the relationships between the
bees and the flowers to the relationships between us and our friends
and family, interactions happen every millisecond of each day. It is
hard to conceptualize a world without relationships. I usually thrive
in the relationships I have with the people in my life; however, this
was not always the case. Much of my pain and trauma came from
those who were closest to me.

Socially, some people prefer to spend their free time alone while
others like to surround themselves with people all the time. Some
prefer to hang out with one or two friends, while others like to be
in big groups. No matter what our preferences are, we build and
strengthen our relationships every time we relate to and interact

with others in positive ways. For children, relationships are super important for growth and development because relationships build and strengthen our brains. They can even help us to live a longer life. If we have traumatic relationships, however, this can negatively affect us in many ways. I have learned it is important for me to take the time to build relationships that are positive and do not bring me down or cause me a lot of stress. My mental health does not do well when I am stressed out in my relationships.

Many times we choose to be in the position of seeing other people, such as hanging out with our friends. Other times, we do not have control over whether we see an individual. For example, when we are at school or work, we are forced to have some sort of relationship with our classmates and coworkers even if we are not fond of them. This is where relationship management skills can really help. We have to learn how to live harmoniously with others, but this does not mean that we have to necessarily like everyone, or that everyone will like us, either.

Something that I have thought a lot about throughout my life is the question of: Why are relationships so fundamentally important to humankind? Why can't I just live my life by myself, and not have to worry about pleasing friends or family members? Why do I have to be around people who seem to care about me, but actually talk about me behind my back? Sometimes, it is hard for me to know who to trust and that is exhausting. Why can't I just live alone? As great as this might sound sometimes, it is not logistically possible. With over seven billion people living on Earth, it is virtually impossible to not see or interact with other people. Most of the time I like to be with others, but this can change based on the day, month or year, and also depends on my mood, stress level, and the state of my mental health at the time.

Our relationships have a huge effect on our mental health, and our mental health also affects our relationships. Our friends and family can help ease our anxiety, but they can also bring stress to the table. Sometimes people help pick us up when we are feeling down, or they can say something that hurts. Relationships can come with love, but I also believe the more you love somebody, the more they are likely to push your buttons and irritate you to no end. Relationships are complex. We can either choose to love people for who they are and learn to embrace people's differences, or just the opposite and fight and be angry. Since we all have different personalities and qualities that make up who we are, no two people will have the same relationships; we all have a web of individuals who make up our circle of people. This shapes us into the unique humans we are.

Relationships can grow stronger when you open up and confide in others, since it shows that you consider them trustworthy and close enough to be honest and upfront about what is going on in your life. Whether we are in a happy mood or feeling at our lowest point, being with others is meaningful to every human being all over the world. Feeling like you have a good support system and people you love and trust makes a big difference in all parts of our lives. It starts with putting yourself out there. Taking risks and learning what works for me with my relationships has not been easy but is getting better all the time. I really appreciate my friends, family, and the other good relationships I have with so many different people.

Feeling like we belong is so important, especially for KGs. It is common when going through the challenges of mental illness to feel like we do not have people to support us or friends that we can trust, and this can make us feel alone and desperate for help. It is difficult to come out of this thought process and remember how many people love and care about our wellbeing. But, when we push ourselves forward and embrace the people we have relationships with, great things can happen. When I am depressed, the only things that I want to do are lay in my bed or lounge around. Most of the time, when I am sad, the last thing I want to do is see my friends or try to look presentable enough to go out and do something fun. Feeling depressed can cause me to isolate, which becomes a vicious cycle of sadness. I believe this can be the case for many KGs. Breaking this cycle is important, because when we are connected with others and utilize our support systems, they help us feel better.

There is a skill in Dialectical Behavior Therapy called "Opposite Action" which encourages us to do the opposite of what our brain wants us to do. For example, when I am sad and feel like isolating myself, the opposite action would be to go talk to somebody and try to get out of my funk. Likewise, when I am anxious about school and feel like staying in and doing all of my work in one night (when it is not due for a month), the opposite action would be to go out and do something fun and get my mind off my stress.

When KGs find our people, it makes a huge difference for our self-esteem. But most of us wonder how to find them. Are "my people" out there? Will I ever have a friend group the way I see others have? It seems like there are so many mean people and fake friends, and sometimes it is difficult to differentiate the real friends from the fake ones. Some people will use you for one thing or another, other friends bail and cancel at the last minute, and sometimes friends just do not seem like they care for you at all. Trying to figure out these types of relationships can be difficult and frustrating.

Add in issues of popularity, or who is in the cooler sorority or club, and it all gets harder to deal with. I hate these things. On top of that, suffering from mental illness and going through times of great anxiety, depression, or trauma can make it harder to socialize in the first place. I know that my anxiety makes me second guess everything I say when I am with people, so having to psychoanalyze myself with people who are not even genuine friends feels like a waste of my energy. I would much rather be with people I know care about me, so I know that they will not judge me if I am a little awkward.

Something that I have been asking myself for a while is if there is any way to identify a real friend from a fake friend in advance. I find that sometimes people may be distant, or they may not seem like they are interested in what I have to say when we are hanging out. It can be hard for me to tell if someone is being a fake friend sometimes. I try to stay true to who I am and not get too caught up in that, and it is easier to keep my perspective when I am in a good space. It is much harder to do when I am struggling.

All relationships are important, but in my opinion, the relationship between an individual and themselves is the most important relationship we will ever have. Like we have discussed in earlier chapters, self-love is not easy. Many people never get to the point where they truly love and accept themselves for who they are. As long as we do not dwell on our imperfections and work on loving ourselves when we are not feeling great, then we are on our way to having a good relationship with ourselves. How can we go around making other people happy when we cannot love ourselves? The more we look in the mirror and accept what we see or say something awkward and accept ourselves anyway, the more we create a positive relationship with ourselves. Beating ourselves up over little imperfections only feeds our depression and brings us down. It is important not to be hard on ourselves, and to recognize and remember how important the relationship we have with ourselves is. We are only given one body in this lifetime, so we need to treat ourselves with kindness and respect and try to enjoy this life we are given.

Relationships are not easy and can be made even harder by the struggles mental illness bring. And, at the same time, we all need others, and we thrive with the love of our closest relationships. Without a doubt, I am the happiest when I am hanging out with my boyfriend and a small group of my real friends by a firepit on a beautiful night. Being able to build healthy relationships and connect with others is worth the time, energy, and the stress that can come along with it.

EXPERT ADVICE

To add more clarity and context to this complex subject of relationships, once again we called upon some powerhouse experts to shed more light on the important topic of relationships.

Dr. Laura Berman is a relationship rock star and an incredible human being. In addition to her many impressive professional accomplishments, including *New York Times* bestselling author, TV personality, and longtime radio host, Dr. Berman is a brilliant, groundbreaking, warm, and generous woman who is committed to helping others. Dr. Berman was an honored guest on our KrazyGirl Project Summer Speakers series produced in 2020 which can be viewed on our website. I am always impressed with Dr. Berman's knowledge, compassion, and humanity.

How we can create and direct the kind of emotional energy we wish to bring into our interpersonal relationships?

At a fundamental level, each of us are pure atomic energy: atoms in a constant but changing vibration. What we now know is that in large part, our bodies' vibrations change with our thoughts and feelings. If you harness your thoughts and feelings and recognize how those feel in your body, you are on your way to harnessing your body's frequency. This is so important because the truth is we are like human tuning forks, constantly (and mostly unconsciously) matching one another's frequency. This is what quantum physicists call 'entrainment.' When we are around others, we 'entrain' to them, meaning we interact with, impact, and naturally match each other's energetic frequency. It is our human nature to try to find a happy medium or balance in this energy. If you are in a yoga class, or a classroom, or on the playground or wherever, your frequency is actually interacting with everyone's energetic frequency, and we all are unconsciously trying to find the happy medium. That is, unless there is someone in the room that is holding a specific frequency and is conscious of doing that. I see this a lot with kids that are anxious or depressed, and almost always these kids are also empaths.

Furthermore, in close relationships we experience what quantum physicists call 'entanglement.' Once two atoms (or system of atoms) are 'entangled,' they are vibrating at the same rate and frequency no matter how far apart they are from one another. If we took two entangled atoms and separated them, even taking one to the moon and leaving the other here, and we changed the rate and frequency of one of the atoms, the other would simultaneously match its entangled partner. Einstein called this 'Spooky action at a distance.' This was the beginning of what is known as quantum physics. Now we are finally beginning to understand how this happens between humans.

An empath actually experiences others' energy and emotions as their own. Many people are anxious and depressed because they are empaths, and they are empaths because they are anxious and depressed. What is happening with an empath on an energetic level? They usually do not have good energetic boundaries at all. Think about what empathy is—putting yourself in place of me. They not only feel deeply (and at times overwhelmingly) what everyone is feeling, but they can't necessarily distinguish their own feelings from others.

In high school, my son Ethan was really depressed and anxious, even suicidal at one point. After trying everything under the sun to help him, I went to a medium. They explained to me that he was clairsentient; that he can't tell the difference between what he was feeling and what everyone else was feeling. That is the struggle of the empath. They come in the house and match the feelings (or energetic frequency) of everyone there, be it their partner or their parents. The other people who are highly empathic are people who grew up in abusive or conflicted households, where they had to learn to be vigilant to the household energy for their own survival.

On a quantum level, what I try to teach people is to start being really conscious of what is energetically theirs and what is someone else's. And to also become more aware of our own conscious and subconscious emotional states and how this can impact others. I had to learn this in order to help Ethan. I had to get control of my own (conscious and unconscious) emotions before I even walked in the room with him. Because what an empath will feel is not only the energy you know you have, but the energy you may not even be aware you are holding. Remember that in our most intimate relationships, with our partner or children, we are energetically entangled with each other. This is what led me to realize I had show people how to master their own frequencies and change the way others showed up around them. Because I can deeply impact my child or my partner's energic state by consciously holding my own frequency, I don't even need to say anything. If I am the one who holds the frequency, they will automatically match that. This is actually a superpower, and you can change the energy of any room you enter by being aware of, harnessing, and holding an intentional energetic frequency yourself.

Also, if we realize that we are feeling a certain feeling, we can ask ourselves if it is me who is feeling this way, or is there someone else close to me that is feeling this way that I am picking up on? This was a big transition for my son, when he learned to distinguish between his own feelings and energy and that of others. From a social success standpoint, which is so important for teens and young adults, learning that we can set a frequency before we walk into a classroom, or go on a date, or have an important conversation with parents is very powerful. If we want something to go well, we are more empowered than we may think, because we can consciously set the frequency in the room, which will impact the outcome we want to create.

We need to connect with each other and to belong. We all need our people . . . There is little that is as important as having a group that supports you, that has a similar view of the world and will remind you that you are not crazy (Krazy), for women and especially for younger women. And I will add that it is beneficial to have people of different ages in your circle. A mentor figure, such as a professor, grandparent, coach, or co-worker can help provide a different viewpoint than a peer. There is something extremely powerful for both the older and the younger person that comes from the perspective of someone at a different stage or place in life from your own. You won't feel this way at sixteen or twenty about your own mother, but there are so many cool, interesting, aspirational older women around, and each can gain so much from the other's energy, life experience, wisdom, and perspective. We also need to have people our same age to understand and connect with. I see this as same-age peers creating a circle of support, and multigenerational age creating a sphere of support. I have friends of all ages and we learn and grow and co-create as a sisterhood together. We all need a sisterhood of love and support, but be selective in choosing this. Those in your circle must have your back. Not that they need to agree with you all the time, but true safety and support has to be there. Your group must contain positive soul mirrors that reflect your highest self. Knowing when to walk away from friends that do not truly support you is hard, but extremely important.

Eric Kispert, LCSW is a bona fide Master RLT certified relationship therapist, my mentor and friend. I am grateful to Eric for his wisdom, humanity, and teachings over some long and hard years of my life. Eric shared some wise thoughts with me on the topic of KGs and relationships during a profoundly enriching conversation I was privileged to enjoy with him.

When I have worked with depressed people, other than psychotropic medication, the best thing we can do to alleviate depression is to be around other human beings. So I often use the example of food courts at malls: If I put a person with depression at a food court for two hours, when I came back they would be less depressed, simply by being in the presence of others. We see this in the early research from orphanages in Eastern Europe. When children were not held, their development was stunted. With the aged, when you put them in an active community—not in bed— they have a higher and better quality of life merely by having connections and a sense of belonging. Individuals who are isolated, we have a word for that. It is usually called depression. I am not talking about introverts, but those who do not find some kind of community in which they affiliate. We have choices whether to belong or not, be it in the local temple, little league, or the rotary. Most of us have some community where we are affiliated, be it spiritually, in the community, or at work. We know it makes us feel better when we belong. Wellness increases as we live in healthy relationships with each other.

The challenge, especially for a sixteen-year-old with issues, is that they usually want most what they feel the least: namely being a part of and connected to a group. Pia Mellody shares that the singular job for parents of sixteen- to twenty-three-year-olds is to keep them alive. Simply because that time of life is so fraught with such helplessness, such loneliness, worthlessness, and inability. It is that catch-22: I am not a cute little kid anymore that everybody wants to fawn all over like when I was eight and nine and my mommy was putting barrettes in my hair. And I am also not twenty-seven with my own job and apartment, launched with my own life. No, it is that distance between childhood and adulthood that at times can be just so crippling. Adolescence for me is like that old saying, 'When God closes a door he opens a window, but being in the hallway is a real bitch!' That to me is saying the doorway is childhood, the window is adulthood, and the hallway is adolescence. The only way to get through it is to get through it. Candidly, for me, I was suicidal and wanted to kill myself much of the time between the ages of seventeen and twenty. I thought about suicide every day. Mostly because I did feel as if I belonged, I did not fit in, I did not feel connected. Even when I was connected, I felt lonely, isolated, worthless. Not that this is every teenager, but most can identify with some aspect of this, whether they are going to Harvard or going to rehab.

What parents can do to help most is to take a healthy dose of patience, hold on tight, and realize that time is our friend. We need to hold the hope for our kids that the adolescent cannot provide for themselves. And when they are running amok, in a hospital or psych program, or so over functioned that they are the class valedictorian or head of the honor society, we need to see that over functioning as a symptom that they feel not good enough or that they do not matter. Not that every smart kid has issues, but let's not deny the fact that really smart kids can also have issues. The parents' role is primarily one of hope. We need to do whatever we need to do to keep ourselves in check, because this time of life is hard on us, too. We can get angry and browbeat or loop in a negative pattern, but that does not help. I like to say that when the kids are small, we put them in time out and when they are teenagers we put ourselves in time out. We need to create space for our own mental wellness before we can even think of being conduits of hope for our children, especially during this period of incredible turbulence called adolescence.

Steven Donohue, MSW, MCLC, is a friend, a social worker, a practicing Master Certified Life Coach and the CEO of Core Four, a consulting and coaching firm. Steve is a congressionally-awarded advocate for Veterans' rights and a published author of the book, *What Every Man Needs to Know.*

The need to belong is natural. Humans are tribal people. We are social beings. We have survived and sprawled this land we call Earth by manifesting ourselves in packs. The concept of family wasn't as fortified in our society, but the need for strength in numbers was. We've changed a bit over time, our strength in numbers is no longer being used to defend ourselves from mammoths and tigers, but now our beasts of burden are the acceptance of our peers. If someone were to ask me what is harder to combat, the creatures, or the burden of approval, I'd say the burden. Why?

If you were able to identify what you had to combat, you'd be able to prepare, learn, and execute a plan of action. This is the method by which you could combat these creatures. On the other hand, as a society and those within it continuously changing, your ability to prepare, learn, and execute is a vital skill. The desire to belong is an innate feeling. But to belong, first you must identify your community and, even more so, determine who you are as a person. The journey towards this realization is not always an overnight success story. You may experience moments of loneliness, pressure, and a sense of feeling lost at this time.

Why would you feel this? As individualistic and unique we are, we are very similar to each other. Think of this example, a boy, age sixteen, moves into a new town. He knows no one, but he enjoys playing sports and plays the drums. These two traits are the boy's identified communities; he can try to attach himself to them and find his place in his new environment. These identified traits set the stage, so now, let's throw in the element of mental illness. The boy struggles with social anxiety and has a history of spending his time alone due to not being accepted by certain people due to his mental illness. His loneliness increases, and his self-esteem decreases; the conflict that ensues is the conflict of wanting to be part of a group and the feeling of not being in one, or so he believes. We always belong to a community; if you have an interest, the group exists. The relationships of a person are often dependent on where they feel the most comfortable.

We don't always identify with the groups available, so we 'act' like we are. Once we recognize who we are and our value system, we no longer live in isolation, but can cut a niche into pre-existing groups. When coping with a mental health diagnosis, directly or indirectly, you're searching for a community and already belong to many.

One community that you're born into and speak to every time you introduce yourself is your family. Your family will influence you much more than your conscious mind will know and, in some cases, accept. The dynamic of the family relationship is integral to the development of a person. Even our views of ourselves are cut from the cloth of our family's belief systems too often. For example, suppose you were raised in a homophobic household, and you identify within the LGBTQ community. In that case, you may be more reluctant to accept who you are or be honest with others around you. You belong to multiple groups at this point, but the one you were raised in does not accept you for your others. This is just one example.

The family dynamic is a broad topic that has enough literature to create debate across many mediums. Still one focus rings true: You are influenced by your family dynamic and potentially will repeat the pattern. One key way to disrupt this cycle is to identify the feelings that you experience within the cycle. Suppose you find yourself feeling anxious, nervous, sad, or angry before seeing your mother or father. In that case, there is a clear indication that there is a negative experience associated with them. Trace the feeling or feelings to the point that validates the feeling based on experience, not just emotion.

You'll begin to find your reasoning, which provides internal validation and evidence that you can provide your *mother and father when you're willing to extend yourself into that conversation. It may seem like a very tall order, but a challenging conversation with a person does not outweigh the burden to bear in the event you live with this extra weight for the rest of your life. Speaking from your truth is just as much a survival tactic as being able to identify poisonous berries in the wild. Have the hard conversations; they pay off the most in the end.*

I challenge you to step back and write three traits about yourself that you identify. Go to Google and type in one of your identified traits. I believe you will find many avenues and communities that exist that think and live the same way. The world is a complex place; travel it in community.

Katharine (Kalo) Maloney, LCSW, is a close friend, and an original member of the Ant Hill Mob Motorcycle Club Ladies Auxiliary alongside me in the 1970s. She has made the most of her interesting and colorful life as an artist, licensed clinical social worker, hospice advocate, educator, and proud mother.

Most people have the human need to connect with others. It is not always an easy thing to do, however, especially if there are mental health issues going on. This is a skill that can be learned and practiced and will help a lot to improve our mental health and wellness. The best way to connect with others is to be interested in them. Ask questions about them—who they are and how they operate in the world. Get to know them and how they may be different or the same as yourself. There was a great YouTube video where people from very different backgrounds were put together in a room. At first, they were all clearly uncomfortable with each other, but then they had to ask each other questions. As they did, you could see them building connections. Over a short amount of time they actually began to build bonds with each other. The safest thing you can do if you are

*feeling vulnerable is to take small steps and build safety
and success through a support group. When my son was
diagnosed with ADHD, I was concerned that I would be
judged as a bad parent. I felt sad, vulnerable, and had a lot
of loss and felt alone. So I went to a support group and that
really helped me to feel connected. I learned and grew in
those connections, and I felt much better. Sometimes we
need a bridge to build ourselves up, and we can move on
to grow other connections from there.*

Beryl Bender Birch, credited for bringing yoga mainstream in the
US in the 1980s, has great wisdom to share regarding yogic ways to
approach mental health and wellness.

Regarding relationships, Beryl feels strongly that being part of
a spiritual community is essential to our well-being. She discusses
"Blue Zones," which are places on the planet where a large percentage
of the population lives to be over one hundred.

*Why do people live so much longer and healthier in Blue
Zones? They all 'connect,' either through family, 'right
tribe,' or being part of a faith-based community. Finding
your 'right tribe,' such as a twelve-step program, a hiking
or walking group, a yoga studio, or any group that inspires
you to be your best self, is important. But more importantly
is your* sangha, *your deep spiritual community of like-
minded souls who are working on their own evolution and
working for the good of the planet. This can also be found
at your local yoga studio, or at your church, your temple, or
through the teachings of any spiritual leader, organization,
or community.*

At their best, relationships are the embodiment of the highest
love that humanity is capable of. A parent fueled by a surge of
adrenaline can lift a car to free their child pinned underneath. A

spouse devotedly stays by the side of their dying partner of sixty years as they cross over to the other side. An artist, poet, or musician funnels emotion from deep within their soul to share their humanity with the world. At our relational worst, we are capable of unspeakable pain and cruelty. Lord Voldemort. Mean girls. Domestic violence. Human relationships matter, and all of us need to feel like we belong. There is no escaping this fact. Whether we reach up and out with love or build impenetrable bricks in our walls for generations to come, the choice of how we relate to others is ours alone to decide.

CHAPTER 7

Family Dynamics
Roll Downhill

"And what about this feeling that I'm never good enough,
will it wash out in the water, or is it always in the blood?"
—John Mayer

"We are family . . . I got all my sisters with me,
Get up everybody and SING!"
—Sisters Sledge

MARCI

Most of us grow up and are shaped within the circle of our family dynamics. Regardless of the form or structure of our family, the seeds of our souls are germinated within this environment. Family traditions, values, and belief systems are both intentionally and unintentionally passed down through generational lines. How a family views and responds to mental health issues within their midst has a huge impact on the recovery process for all involved.

The family is a dynamic system, much like a spoked wheel. The wheel functions best when all the spokes are strong. If one spoke becomes compromised, the entire wheel begins to wobble. Other spokes might try to pick up the slack, but if unchecked, the wheel will eventually break down. At the same time, if there is a problem with the structure of the wheel itself, each spoke will also be affected. *The parts affect the whole, and the whole affects the parts.* The more we can understand the implications of these processes, the more we can intentionally work with them for the betterment of ourselves, our loved ones, and for future generations to come.

I have always been fascinated by the question of how we come to be the people we are. From the time I was young and became aware that I had a PsychoDad who was not the father that raised me, I grappled with this issue. As far back as I can remember I tried to make sense of who I was within the context of my family, school, friends, religion, and ultimately, myself. I was curious about the role of *nature,* which is what we inherit biologically and who we are on a cellular level. I also considered the role of *nurture,* which involves environmental influences and how those we grew up with shaped our personality. I wondered how these and other factors could contribute to and ultimately create our essential beings.

As I grew as a person, and as a family therapist, I looked deeper into the role of the factors that are involved in the business of how family dynamics roll downhill. I have come to see the role of the development of our Parts and the True Self, Individuation, Conditioned Responses, The Laws of Homeostasis, and Family Attitudes and Beliefs (FABs[9]) as the main factors that are involved in this process. I continue to try to understand and work with these divergent forces to assist the individuals and families I work with and myself, in consciously understanding and directing what destiny has bestowed upon us all.

---

9   Ober, 2021

Nature Versus Nurture

Let's dig deeper into the concept of nature vs. nurture. *Tabula rasa* is a term that literally means "blank slate."[10] When I was an undergraduate psychology student, it was my firm belief that we are all born into a neutral state of being—essentially blank slates coming into the world, awaiting the influence of our parents and environments to shape us. This was long before there was any such thing as the internet, the human genome project, 23andMe, or any of the other methods now widely available to test for and understand the role of our human genetics.

My graduate training as a family therapist in the late 1980s followed the great minds of the original family therapy movement. This included Murray Bowan, who developed the *genogram*[11] to map the transmission of family traits from generation to generation. A genogram looks for repeated family patterns, such as addiction, infidelity, abandonment, abuse, love bonds, alliances, and other family characteristics and recurring themes. Part of my training was to conduct an in-depth genogram on myself and the other students in the cohort. Talk about a light bulb moment! Like John Mayer sings . . . *"How much of my mother has my mother left in me? How much of my love will be insane to some degree . . . "* Seeing, on paper in front of my eyes, traits of my family being passed down and repeated throughout generations was overwhelming and confirmed my bias that family dynamics must be created by nurture. However, this was a snapshot in time of my evolution as a family therapist, and looking back, was limited in scope and somewhat naive.

In 1991, when I was twenty-nine, I had the opportunity to move to Anchorage, Alaska, where I lived and worked for seven years. Anchorage is a fascinating place. It is the largest city, in the largest

10   Noun, "an absence of preconceived ideas or predetermined goals, a clean slate", Websters.
11   A genogram is a detailed multi-generational diagram, usually collected in therapy, to understand and highlight family dynamics that have rolled down-hill, including mental health issues, alliances, cut-off's, etc.

state in the nation, with a total population of approximately 225,000 residents the year I moved there. To put this in context, the entire state at the time I was there had an overall population of only about 569,000—in a geographical area five times the size of Texas. It is an enormous, wild, and isolated place. There are two cities—Anchorage and Fairbanks, a sprinkling of small towns, and a multitude of Native Alaskan villages. The topography of this amazing state includes coastal, arctic, mountainous, or literally frozen over and devoid of light for nearly half the year. The sheer distance between towns and villages renders many villages isolated, and of course, prior to the 1990s, the internet was not yet a thing. Therefore, many communities existed cloistered together, completely undisturbed by outside influences, for generations. Based on these factors, tribal villages adapted to their environments and developed well-defined, specific, and unique ways of living and relating to the world.

I worked as a family therapist, and then as clinical director, at the only dedicated psychiatric hospital in the state. There, I came up close and personal with multigenerational family dynamics from a brand-new perspective, which made me question the role of nature vs. nurture even more. Doing intense, hospital-based family therapy in this setting, I learned about cultural characteristics and belief systems that were entirely different from my own, or from each other. Athabaskan, Aleut, Eskimo, Inuit, Yupik, Tlingit, Haida. Based on the village and tribal affiliation of the families, dominant traits and characteristics became clearly identifiable. Some families were naturally more open and accepting of assistance, while others could be hostile, combative, or refuse treatment entirely. There were clear differences between groups in terms of gender roles, eye contact, body language, willingness to participate in therapy, family hierarchy patterns, or use of money. To conduct effective therapy, I needed to be able to relate with warmth and understanding to whomever was sitting on my couch. Fortunately, my therapy was informed and shaped by the kind assistance of an Alaska native coworker, who patiently coached me in tribal etiquette and therapeutic strategies likely to be embraced. I got to participate in some wonderful new (to me) healing techniques, such as the use of smudging, talking circles, invoking ancestors, or collaborating with a shaman or tribal elder, who were the backbone of healing in many of these off-grid communities.

As each of our patients was reviewed in daily treatment team meetings, doctors, nurses, therapists, and social workers considered the role of both nature *and* nurture in providing the best clinical treatment possible. This was a delicate process: what parts of individual family dynamics were healthy or dysfunctional for the patient when considered within a cultural context? What was the significance of family attitudes and beliefs that could be contributing to depression, addiction, psychosis, or abuse patterns? What therapeutic interventions could facilitate long-term healing and recovery for our hospitalized children, teens, their families, and communities?

Reflecting back, I feel so fortunate to have been part of such an amazing team of caring professionals at NorthStar Hospital in the 1990s. It was clear that we made a positive difference in the lives of our patients and their communities. Appreciation of our efforts were demonstrated in grateful offerings of *muktuk,* which is whale blubber, a delicacy and gift of great significance, or other heartfelt and unusual expressions of gratitude. I will never forget the lessons I learned about the role of both biology *and* family influence within the structure of diverse communities and cultures.

Each of us contains a unique blend of traits, characteristics, attitudes, and beliefs, that are learned and also biologically driven. We are destined to pass along our family dynamics to our children and to future generations. Some of these will be shared intentionally, some lie beneath our consciousness, and some are locked deep within our neurobiology and DNA.

The Business of the Family

The concept that "family dynamics roll downhill" means that inherited familial characteristics, both biological and environmental, will likely continue on to our children and beyond unless they are identified and intentionally redesigned. Most families deliberately pass down thoughtful and positive traditions, such as holiday traditions, family dinners, recipes, vacations, bedtime rituals, and values relating to education, work, and morality. These are largely positive experiences that are beneficial to all involved. However, there are also dysfunctional patterns that can get passed on, frequently without awareness of their existence. This is not unlike the biblical term, "The sins of the father shall be visited upon the sons," or a sneaky virus that hacks our account and causes chaos and destruction. Sometimes we understand issues and challenges that were passed down through our family. However, if this is a new concept, it is worth opening up to the role of unfinished family business and how it can contribute to or maintain mental health problems. When we understand how dysfunctional family patterns roll downhill and we can alter the course, there is great potential for positive change exactly where it is needed the most.

To illustrate, consider this scenario: Mary comes from a home where parental alcoholism deeply affected her childhood. She is sensitive to the fact that alcoholism also affected her mother's life growing up, but her mom unwittingly repeated the pattern by marrying an alcoholic who was very much like her own father. As Mary starts to consider marriage, she looks at how her boyfriend uses alcohol, determined to avoid repeating this painful family legacy. That brave acknowledgment and determination to change course can prevent this pattern from repeating again in the family she creates. Additionally, when her future children become teenagers, she lets them know that alcoholism runs in the family bloodline, cautioning them to be careful because they are at risk for problem drinking due to their biology. If we blindly adopt and perpetuate dysfunctional family patterns, we continue the cycle in some way, shape, or form. When we become aware of unfinished family business and intentionally choose to do things differently, we can redirect the course of history.

Parts Party and the True Self

There is a school of psychotherapy called Parts-Therapy, or Self-Therapy. This work is based on the concept that the human personality is made up of different aspects, or parts, that live deep within our subconscious minds. The goal of this style of therapy is to identify and develop a relationship with each part, so it becomes understood, given a voice, and integrated into the overall self. Parts are thought to originate from our family of origin[12] and other formative experiences, and are essentially the internalized voices of our parents or other influential role models, or are younger versions of ourselves, also known as our inner child.

A well-functioning adult cannot allow an individual part to have the authority to unilaterally make important life choices. This is the domain of the True Self. Ideally, the True Self functions like a wise and loving parent, who hears and understands all the parts, but would not let a five-year-old having a temper tantrum drive the family car. I share with my patients that I see this process similar to a skillful conductor leading an orchestra. Each instrument is distinct and has a role in the orchestra, but the way in which the music is played comes through the experienced hand of the conductor. The higher functioning the true self is, the more we can artfully conduct the orchestra of our lives, and not allow a single instrument to dominate the entire orchestra.

Individuation and Conditioned Responses

Individuation is the process by which a person achieves their own sense of identity, separate and distinct from the identities of others. In essence, we grow, develop, and become our own person. This concept is similar to the development of the True Self. Many child development models exist that discuss the stages of human psychological development, and we know that individuals continue to grow and evolve throughout childhood, adolescence, and adulthood. However, unfinished family

---

12   The family we came from, this is a common term in the family therapy world.

business and underdeveloped parts, can hamper the individuation process and support unhealthy conditioned response patterns.

A conditioned response is a reaction that automatically occurs, as a result of a cause-and-effect experience over time. For example, Johnny gets badly burned touching the flame on the stove. This experience leads to fear and intense desire to avoid all fire. The parents see this conditioned response and intentionally resolve it through patiently teaching about fire safety. The child is still cautious, but no longer overwhelmed by fear of fire. If that trauma had not been resolved, it could have led to a lifelong phobia. We all live under the influence of our conditioned responses, some positive, some negative, and these experiences set the stage for how we relate to ourselves, others, and the world at large. When we become aware of these patterns and become aware of how they play out in our lives, we can decide to continue down the same path, or change course.

Homeostasis

Sometimes, despite our best efforts at positive change, we bump into a brick wall. Homeostasis, or the force of resistance to change, is a scientific term that explains the process of balance and equilibrium that exists within all systems. Think of this like a pebble that falls into a smooth-surfaced, still pond. There will be ripples for a short while, but soon the pond returns to its previously calm surface. As the laws of physics dictate, things resist change when no forces are acting upon them. Individuals and families are influenced by the laws of homeostasis, like any other system. This means that the tendency will always be to *go back to how it used to be* unless a sustained force continues to move things in a different direction. Recognizing this tendency is important, because changing conditioned responses takes intentional sustained effort. To be successful in creating change, we must take into account the homeostatic forces that will push back on us, and not let them derail our progress.

Family Attitudes and Beliefs (FABs)[13]

Nature, nurture, unfinished family business, parts, conditioned responses, and homeostasis are some of the mechanisms of how family dynamics roll downhill. When we are aware of these factors, it helps us to move forward and create intentional, and potentially lasting, change. The next steps involve identifying our specific Family Attitudes and Beliefs (FABs), and then creating an action plan to address them. Shifting dysfunctional or stuck family dynamics works best, with an open mind at what is happening both inside and outside ourselves.

The following concept bank can raise awareness of potential issues you may want to think about addressing. These are some of the most common issues and themes that I see people working on in therapy, to improve their relational health.

FAB Concept Bank

Consider the following areas. Do you recognize any repeated patterns or struggles that play out in your personal or family dynamic? Can you trace anything to your formative years, or Family Attitudes or Beliefs (FABs)? The stories that exist around many of these common themes have their basis in the struggles our ancestors experienced. Unresolved in previous generations, they are handed down the family line in the form of FABs, and many live on, long beyond any useful shelf life they might have originally held. Consider the topics below. Does anything stand out that you may want to take a closer look at?

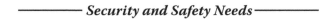

———————— Security and Safety Needs ————————

Maslow's hierarchy of needs is a model that resembles a pyramid and looks at the role of human needs. According to Maslow, we can't move on to higher-order needs until we are secure in the lower levels, since each builds on the success of the previous ones. At the base

---

13   Ober 2021

of the pyramid lies the most basic of human safety needs including food, water, rest, and shelter. We need to be secure in these areas to move on, for if we are not, we get stuck and cannot progress. The next level involves our security needs, such as employment, property, and health. The level after that includes love and belonging needs, such as friendship, intimacy, and connection to others. The next level involves areas of esteem, including respect, self-esteem, recognition, status, and freedom. At the very top of the pyramid is self-actualization, which means to evolve into the best humans we are capable of being. If we come from a family background where scarcity in the lower levels was a dominant issue, this can impact us throughout our lives and can even be passed down to future generations.

If you come from a background where basic survival needs were lacking, how does this issue affect you now? What are your FABs about security and safety? Are those attitudes and beliefs appropriate to your here and now life circumstances? This also can closely relate to the following issue of money and finances.

Money and Finances

Money is a highly personal topic, and we usually don't think a lot about where our FABs around money and financial concerns come from. Take a moment and consider your very first money memory. How old were you, and how did that experience with money feel to you at the time? Does that experience continue to influence you? What was/is your family's relationship toward money? Do they tend to save for a rainy day or spend it while they can? What FABs around money do you have, and why?

Centripetal Versus Centrifugal
(Innie or Outie Family)

Centripetal families see the family, and often the larger extended family, as the most important source of life satisfaction. This word actually means to *circle inward* or move to the center. Centripetal families could believe, for example, that Sunday dinner is a must-attend, kids should never go away to sleep away camp, or that going to college is OK, as long as you don't go too far from home. Centrifugal families are more outwardly focused. Think of centrifugal force as the energy that propels things outward. Centrifugal families believe that many of the riches life has to offer exist outside the family, in the world. For example: FAB's may include the belief that young adults should move out and go start their life, it is good to go away to camp, or please pick the college you want to attend, even if it is far away from home. Neither approach is better or worse than the other, but they are vastly different ways of experiencing life. FABs of this type are often deeply embedded within family culture, and can be a great source of conflict when combined with a mate who comes from an opposite-style family.

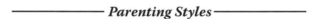

Parenting Styles

There are four parenting styles according to a study in the *Journal of Child and Family Studies*. These include **Authoritative**, **Passive**, **Authoritarian**, and **Uninvolved**. The study presents two intersecting axes: discipline and parental involvement. The intersection between how discipline is handled (heavier or lighter), and parental involvement (low to high) create a dominant *parenting style*. Authoritative parents who have a high level of parental involvement, and also provide strong discipline were found to be the most effective. Passive parents provide lower discipline and high parental involvement (more like a friend), which was found to be less effective. Authoritarian parents are high on the discipline side and low on parental involvement. They are controlling, expect obedience, and are less warm with their kids, which was also found to be less effective. Uninvolved parents do not provide much discipline or parental involvement. They can be less warm, absent, or reject their children, which was found to be the least effective style of parenting. Consider the parenting style(s) in the home you grew up in. What about your spouse? What are your FABs regarding parenting styles? Is there conflict or room for improvement in your current family dynamic?

Communication Patterns

How does your family communicate? Is there a lot of yelling? Do people impose the silent treatment on each other when they are upset? Are difficult issues typically avoided, or is communication clear, direct, and easy to understand? Are messages sent indirectly, through sarcasm, or through other family members, (*go and tell your father . . .*)? Are children to be seen and not heard? Are problems effectively resolved through communication, or do things linger or remain unresolved? Do you tend to communicate like a particular member of your family of origin, or have you taken on the patterns of one or more of your parents? What FABs do you have regarding communication patterns?

Love Relationships

How did your parents get along with each other when you were growing up? Were they divorced or married? Were they happy together, did they struggle to get along, or were they downright hostile toward one another? What did you come to believe about love relationships? What stories about love continue to play out in your closest intimate relationships? How have your FABs manifested in your choice of partners, or how relationships progress forward? What would you like to improve upon in this area?

Secrets/Shame/Blame

Were there any skeletons in your family closet or shameful family secrets? Do you know where they came from and why they existed? Were there things at home that the neighbors couldn't know about?

Was there a wrong that was never righted within your family tree? Is there anger or blame toward any group or entity that still exists? What is the effect of this unfinished family business upon your current life?

Power

Who had the real power in your home? How was that power used? Was there a certain brother or sister who held more influence than the others? Did mom provide effective discipline, or did she wait for dad to come home? Maybe there was a grandma or an elder who held the real power in the family? How did this affect you? If you could change the balance of power in your family, what would you do? How does this relate to your FABs about power today?

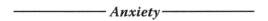

Anxiety

Was one or both of your parents or close extended family members an anxious person? Were there strongly held superstitions or taboos in the home while you were growing up? What kinds of things did that involve, such as prohibitions or phobias that held strong emotional energy? How did that affect you? FABs around anxiety can have a profound effect on our current response patterns and how we go about our lives. This can often involve a somewhat irrational internalized fear or strong behavioral dictates and can seem to suddenly emerge when we have our own children.

Parental Self-Absorption

What was expected from you around fulfilling your parents' expectations (*my son the doctor!*)? Was your performance on the field, at work or school, or in your choice of relationships heavily influenced by your parents' demands and expectations? How did/do you respond to this? Comply? Rebel? Give up? What FABs do you hold onto as a result?

Religion

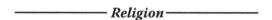

Do you come from a strong religious or spiritual background? What was, or continues to be, the effect of religion on you? Do you feel enriched or connected within a religious community? Or are there expectations you feel you must live up to, or that you struggle with? Are there FABs around religion you would like to examine or re-work in some way? It is common to feel guilty or disloyal around themes of religion and family expectations. Be gentle with yourself and try to obtain the support of someone you trust who also comes from the same or similar religious background if you chose to go deeper into this area.

Sex

The topic of sex is a hot button issue in many, if not most, family households. Sex before marriage, sex for pleasure, masturbation, teenage sex, and birth control all have strong connotations, and children are usually raised with their parental guidelines firmly in place. At the same time, young people often make sexual choices that differ from the values of their parents, religion, or culture. What FABs did your family hold and/or express regarding sex? Are there any issues that remain challenging or feel like they are unfinished business around sex for you?

Sex Roles and Birth Order

The very first indication of the value an individual holds is frequently based on their sex and their birth order. A firstborn son is often the crowning achievement in the life of a young family and his arrival is usually celebrated. Maybe not so much for future children. Males typically hold more power in a family dynamic, and male children can have more influence than even adult females do, depending on cultural norms. Birth order also can influence the power and authority a person holds within their family and community. There can be strong FABs related to sex roles and birth order. Is this an area where family business has a current effect on you, your self-esteem, or the relationship dynamics that play out in your relationships today?

Substances of Use and Abuse

Alcohol, marijuana, and other drugs are a fact of life, in most if not all societies. As far back as exists in recorded history, there is evidence that native and aboriginal peoples used plants and herbs to alter mood and human biology. FABs vary greatly in their approach to the use or abuse of substances. This can range from totally taboo, to mild or acceptable usage under certain circumstances, to recreational use, to abuse, or addiction. How were alcohol or drugs viewed in the home you grew up in? Was/is your viewpoint aligned or divergent from the family and the culture you grew up in? Is this an area that needs some focus, as you think about your own inherited family attitudes and beliefs?

Food

Food equals life. Our first experiences with food can set the stage for our lifelong relationship with food. Food can be many things: comfort, love, sustenance, pleasure, recreation, family rituals, anesthesia. Food can also conjure up issues of scarcity, insecurity, disgust, or anxiety. How food was managed in our family of origin often has a large influence on the role food plays in our lives today. Is body size largely emphasized in the family you come from? What FABs might you hold about food? Is this an area that would benefit you to think about perhaps rebalancing?

Work and Career

Work is another area where families can view things differently. Work can be seen as a job that pays the bills, a level of status and identity obtained through a career path, or anything in between.

There is large variance in how work-life balance is regarded, and strong beliefs exist relating to moms who work or stay at home raising their children. Males and females may have been raised with different expectations and family dictates about working life. What FABs existed in your family about work, and what expectations were placed on you or your siblings in this regard?

Are there any other FAB's you can identify, that affect you and are worthy of consideration?

Family Dynamics Change Exercise: An Eight-Step Process for Freedom

The following exercise is designed to use the FABs you have identified as areas to potentially work on, and begin to consciously interact with them. As you consider each question, try to be as open-minded and curious as possible. Invite the truth that lives deep within you to come forward.

Use the information you got from the FAB concept bank to answer the questions below. Remember, change is a challenging process but is also courageous, rewarding, and empowering. When we understand ourselves more clearly, we can intentionally direct our thoughts, feelings, and behavioral responses the way we choose to and not continue to react to the conditioned responses of unfinished family business.

Questions

Put aside ten minutes and commit some intentional time to do this exercise. Take a nice, deep, cleansing breath and then consider the following questions. Courtney and I have done this exercise and I have provided examples below each question to help you get started.

1. **What is an ongoing FAB issue that negatively affects me (or my KG) that is likely inherited?**

    Marci: I think the feeling of being less valuable than others has been an ongoing issue that has deeply affected my life. Even though I knew my parents loved me, I never felt I really belonged in my family. I felt like my sisters had more value than I did, or that I just was too much work to handle. I was always trying to get validation or attention that was never forthcoming.

    Courtney: I feel as though both sides of my family have mental illness, specifically anxiety, in many forms. Self-judgment, obsessive-compulsive disorder, and worrying about the future or the past are all things that I feel like I inherited from my parents, and these things negatively affect me on a day-to-day basis. I see both of my parents struggling with some of these issues, and I try to understand where I may have adopted these things.

2. **What is the effect of this FAB trait or issue on me or my KG? Be specific.**

    Marci: I think my own insecurities transferred onto my kids. If I was more secure in myself and my social relationships, I think I would have given my kids a stronger sense of self, and better social skill to navigate their tough teenage years. My ish definitely rolled downhill here.

    Courtney: Having anxiety makes me feel bad about myself because oftentimes the worrying does not stop. There are days where I get really caught up in my anxiety and my OCD and I can spend my whole day focusing and dwelling on these things. I do not like when this happens because it feels like my mental illness is getting the best of me.

3. **Where might this trait have originated and what purpose might it have served?**

    Marci: Honestly, I think this trait came from unfinished business from my family line, and we may have compensated by using intellectual accomplishments to make up for underlying insecurity. Not knowing my biological father or anyone on his line at all did not help me feel grounded or secure in myself. My adopted father's parents did not treat me like I belonged in the family. And then I internalized these feelings of worthlessness, by acting out, thereby reinforcing this outsider identity in many different ways.

    Courtney: I could see this trait originating in my parents, possibly as a way to get things done. Sometimes anxiety can be motivating. In the past, my grandmother and great-grandmother might have used anxiety to help them make sure they stayed on track with everything in their lives, such as money. They also could have used their anxiety to help them to relocate to a better homeland. This being said, I do not think anyone wants to have anxiety or face these awful feelings, but it can push the individual to do the things that they are worried about, which can serve a good purpose.

4. **What specific change would be helpful for me to make, to move toward a healthier life?**

    Marci: I am working on creating the most authentic relationships I can for myself at this point in my life. I try to step away from false relationships or places where I do not feel understood or valued. Regardless of the nature or length of a relationship, if it is not authentic or does not support me, I try to minimize them in my life now. I also try to work on my end of insecurity though self-validation and giving grace to the imperfections we all possess.

Courtney: *The changes that I need to make include not letting anxiety and worry get the best of me, as they often do, and not letting them run and control my life. When a thought comes up, doing my best to push back on it or redirect myself and not let it consume me is a good place to start. It takes dedication and hard work to do this but I feel as though these days I am capable of stopping the negative effects that anxiety have on me, for the most part. Although this is always a work in progress.*

5. **If I make this change, will I pay a price or get pushback from others? How?**

Marci: *Perhaps. This remains to be seen. Time will tell. I am ready for whatever happens.*

Courtney: *I definitely will not get any pushback from my family, and I do not think there would be a price for me to pay. This decision would help and benefit me, and I do not see any negative effects attached to making these changes in my life. I think that it would only help make me a better and more positive and present human.*

6. **Create a simple affirmation phrase to repeat to yourself, to help reinforce this change.**

Marci: I have intrinsic value and deserve love, support, understanding and connection. I invite this into my life, and I chose to see and remove all impediments to this in all my personal relationships.

Courtney: I will not let myself get consumed by my thoughts. I am strong and I do not let negative thoughts or worry get in my way.

EXPERT ADVICE

Dr. Laura Berman, the *New York Times* bestselling author we heard from in Chapter Six about relationships, discusses family dynamics and how patterns can be passed along from generation to generation.

Family Dynamics are passed down on multiple levels. There are fascinating recent studies that support the idea that **trauma, not just mood disorders and anxiety, exist in the cellular memory, and are passed down from generation to generation.** *This is not just genetic predisposition which we have understood for decades, but moods, tendencies, and traumatic memories that are stored in the cellular memory. It's in our DNA, a genetic predisposition. This is also transmitted in the family culture, through nurture. Children, grandchildren, and even great-grandchildren of Holocaust survivors are good examples of this. What your great-grandparents experienced, and how your grandparents and parents were raised, and therefore the way you were raised; those subtle messages are transmitted. Whether* *it comes in the form of helicopter parenting, anxiety, overprotectiveness, or the belief that the world is not a safe place, those subtle and sometimes not so subtle messages in a million small and large ways are transmitted through the culture that you are raised in. Other messages such as 'you should be grateful' or 'you should be ashamed' or 'don't get too comfortable' are family ethics that often come out of trauma and pain even if it is several generations back, shaping us in deep ways. There is also evidence that a mother, while gestating her baby, is bathing her child in the same neurochemicals that she herself is experiencing while pregnant. That baby comes into the world with this same neuropeptide predisposition, so our bodies are essentially born addicted to certain moods. There is complex physiology involved, but we build receptors for these same neurochemicals that we are used to, and this process perpetuates. So there are lots of ways that family dynamics get replicated and transmitted. How conflict is handled within the family structure, or how independence is handled, all of those things will definitely influence us.*

I asked Dr. Berman about her latest book, *Quantum Love*, and how this relates to transmitted family dynamics:

We are born high-frequency beings. Even if we have a predisposition toward certain mood states, we are born very pure. Very quickly, however, because it is part of our survival, we pick up on and interpret our parents' messages about what emotional states are acceptable. Because babies are deeply dependent on their caretakers, they get immediate feedback about the responsiveness or engagement of their caretakers and what is and is not acceptable. Depending on the repeated feedback they get, they learn about how much aliveness or joy is allowed in the family. This is called emotional set points, and they come from the overt, conscious, or even unconscious messages we repeatedly receive while growing up, based on our parents' own emotional set points.

How can we intentionally change the family dynamics we have inherited?

The first step is awareness of the "worthiness killing stories" that exist within our families. These are stories that we adopt about what to expect from love, and our worthiness of love. If you think about these stories in a general sense, such as "all men leave," or "all men cheat," what you will generally find is that the same theme or story is repeated in your mother, or grandmother, and so on, and these stories may come from different catalysts. Many times, this story may not even be told out loud, but they are the attitudes or beliefs that came from somewhere back in the family line.

Parenting experts say that it is more important what parents do than what they say because children internalize the beliefs that their parents hold. We need to question our limiting beliefs or the stories we have inherited about what we deserve or are worthy of; those stories that stand in the way of creating what we want in our lives. Talk to your mother and grandmother about this, or just think about what you know about their lives and what they went through that may have led to these stories. For example, if someone is shy, they can ask who else in the family is shy, or what is the family story around shyness? We need to get to the fear because it is always about fear. At the core of that fear there probably is a story about fear that many in the family also hold, maybe not in exactly the same way but in some variation. Like fear about messing up, or the fear of failure, or the fear of scarcity or losing everything, or being abandoned. This fear probably goes back in the family line and when we change this for ourselves, we also change this for the future and also for the past, because on the quantum level there is no such thing as linear time. Getting clear about family lineage and what has led to attitudes and beliefs is a first step in changing them, because you can't change what you are not aware of.

Then, it's all about making a decision to shift and change and create your own stories, which is a kind of deconditioning. This involves recognizing what your triggers are and where they come from. Expect that you will have a certain body response due to these triggers because there is a neurochemical cascade that happens. The goal is to create a wider pause between action and reaction. As we practice we can increasingly call ourselves to consciousness, and not just go with the flow of our conditioned responses. The more we practice this, the more we can move into a higher home frequency, and this becomes more natural as we work with it over time through conscious effort. The key is recognizing our patterns and triggers and moving to a different and more desirable frequency pattern over time with practice. This is how we can change our family dynamics.

Kalo (Katharine) Maloney, LCSW, is a lifelong friend of mine. You can see a young version of Kalo in the picture of the Ant Hill Mob Ladies Auxiliary in Marci's Story. Kalo is an OGKG (original KrazyGirl) who has also had her own long and winding road to wellness. Kalo put herself through college as a single mother and went on to earn her social work degree and professional license in her middle life years. Her wisdom, compassion, and practical approach to life are rare in this world. I absolutely treasure Kalo.

A family is a system. The parents are the leaders and we learn our roles, how to feel, cope and behave from our parents. They are our primary caretakers and first teachers. They pass down emotional regulation, norms, and values to us. We learn how to treat ourselves and others from how our parents do it. We then go out in the world and try these things out on others and see how they react. It can be very challenging to try to change some of these things, as they are deeply ingrained in us. We tend to be more comfortable with those who do the dance as we do. And that gets passed down from generation to generation. The way we can manage these traits is to become more self-aware and learn to direct these inherited aspects in ourselves.

Becoming self-aware is key. If we can learn to see ourselves with a critical and compassionate eye, we can change what isn't working. We have to be able to acknowledge when we have made a mistake and try to do things differently. Like physical therapy, this may not be a comfortable process, but it is certainly well worth it. If we have enough practice and positive results, change will happen. Set a small goal and intentionally work toward it. For example, we may become aware that we tend to have angry responses as our default reaction. We may think, 'I wish I didn't always strike out (verbally or physically) because it's hurting my (valued) relationship.' If we have the capacity to recognize that, or if it's pointed out to us and we can comprehend it, then we can think about it, and brainstorm other more acceptable responses that may bring better outcomes, and try those and practice them. Not everybody will choose to do this because it is really hard. Only you can decide if the goal of change is worth the uncomfortable process of change.

Dr. Danica Anderson, Ph.D., is a social scientist and a forensic psychologist who specializes in trauma, war crimes, and violence against women in countries such as Afghanistan, Bosnia, Sub-Saharan Africa, Sudan, and Haiti. She is founder of The Kolo: Women's Cross-Cultural Collaboration, an international women's advocacy organization that focuses on resources for self-sustainability within native communities, and healing from trauma resulting from sexual assault, torture, starvation, poverty, and violent events.

Trauma is intensified learning. It is not a mental illness. Survival mechanisms are not to be thrown away. Trauma shows up in social upheavals, trauma events, death/sudden death, and catastrophic illnesses. Pain comprises physical, emotional, and feeling states. There are two ways this can be experienced. One is through survival mechanisms: fight or flight, the flood of cortisol and corresponding hormones input to the body, which affects our capacity to connect to emotions, feelings, and connection of our pain/suffering to feelings. An example of this is burnout, which occurs mentally as well as physically. It is helpful to ask ourselves if we need to survive right now? Or do we need to thrive/flourish? Thriving and flourishing mechanisms result in enhanced and elevated growth, creating energized support towards evolving pathways. Pain/suffering is compassionately and communally understood, as a message that 'we are alive.' Connecting emotions to feelings is a strong pattern of healing, and our health and wellbeing improve as a result.

This is a radically different thought process and approach to understanding and healing trauma and multigenerational family dynamics. While most of us will never face the devastating events that Dr. Anderson helps people heal from, her unique perspective on healing, health, and growth can benefit us all.

The concept of epigenetics, which refers to the body and mind's ingrained ability to adapt and function based on environmental challenges, relates to how family dynamics roll downhill. Dr. Anderson shares:

We are shaped by our environment, and our environment shapes us. Throughout the generations, this process of epigenetics takes place. Only when we become aware that we can actually flip the switch from survival mode, to thrive and flourish mode, can real empowerment towards positive and self-directed change occur. The concept of neuroplasticity means that as we consciously direct our personal growth, our biology will change and begin to accommodate new information and change the ways we relate to ourselves, others, and the world at large. This is incredibly encouraging. Although we may be the recipients of many aspects of intergenerational 'spam,' we all have the ability to reflect upon and interpret these things according to how we live life daily and what our ancestors lived experiences were. This is the path forward towards a better life experience for ourselves, our children, and future generations.

COURTNEY

Most people grow up in a household with people whom they call their family, whether with biological parents, extended family members, or another person who nurtures and assists in development. We're instilled with our parents' genes—something that we are never able to rid ourselves of. Growing up, our mental wellbeing also depends largely on this family structure. If we experience a tough family life, it will make it more difficult for us to be happy inside, and likewise for us to grow and thrive in school, or any other areas of our lives. All members of a family have an effect on each other, like a well-oiled machine. When all the parts are turning in the right direction, there is an equilibrium, and good things are likely to occur, but when the gears shift, things can go haywire. As a KrazyGirl, understanding these family dynamics is crucial to living happily within our family environment.

Nature and nurture directly explain the impacts that the family structure has on an individual. While nature refers to our genetic inheritance, and the things we directly receive from our parents within our DNA, nurture deals with the external factors from our family, such as how we are raised, or moral compass, values, and our culture. I can see how nature and nurture have affected my life, and more specifically, how these elements have shaped me as a person.

When I think about the "nature traits" I have received from my parents in terms of my mental health, I believe that my anxiety and OCD have probably come from my mother (since it exists in her family's history) and my addictive personality and depressive tendencies probably came from my dad. I have never believed myself to look like either of my parents, physically. It is clearer for me to see how the different aspects of my mental illness can be traced back to other family members down my genetic line. It is hard to see a parent struggle with anything, including mental health and addiction problems. Throughout my life, I have seen my mom get stuck on things that bother her, and I can see this habit within myself, too. This is likely a source of my obsessive thoughts, and how I tend to have a hard time moving on from anything without a resolution. Likewise, it has been tough to see my father battle with addiction throughout my lifetime, and I can see that trait within myself too. This is why I make sure to be aware of these things, since they are in my blood, so to speak, and I try to rise up and not give into these thoughts or behaviors.

My "nurture traits," on the other hand, were learned from my parents. I think that my perfectionism, attention to detail, humor, lovingness and compassion, affection, helpfulness, the ability to fix things and comfort with technology come from my dad. My dedication to intellectual tasks, love for learning, organizational habits, hard work ethic, ability to give advice, and deep interest in psychology and studying the human mind have all come from my mother. I am thankful for the various traits my parents have given and instilled in me, both the positives and the negatives. I work to use everything they have taught me over the years to grow and develop into the best version of myself.

Not only do children inherit traits and genetics from their parents, but they also develop conditioned responses and behaviors. From everyday things like getting hotheaded about certain actions of others, or starting a task the minute I receive it, I have certainly adopted some of my family members' responses. This is primarily unintentional, resulting from being so close to them for so many years. These responses can help me when they bring positivity into my world or be detrimental when they cause harm to myself or others. Regardless, I work to keep the things that benefit me while letting go of the habits that do not serve.

Living within a family, no matter how chaotic and unstable or organized and secure, is a difficult task. Being around people, without choosing to do so, for any period of time, is hard! We get frustrated with one another. We can be best friends one day and enemies the next. We squabble and argue and then have to sit in the same room. These are all aspects unique to the family structure. Sometimes our family members can make us our happiest, and other times they can make us so angry we cannot think straight. Even worse—they may cause harm to our mental wellbeing. Also, we can be frustrated with what our family has instilled in us, such as genetic traits, values, morals, or even religious and spiritual affiliations. But this is why us KGs need to acknowledge all the things our family has given us and work to make the best with what we have. Only then can we grow and flourish as individuals.

I am so thankful to have had such an amazing family and to have genuine and kind people in my life. But not everyone has it so easy. I'm so grateful that I can relate with my mother so well we can collaborate to write this book. She is truly my best friend, and although I am angry with her sometimes, I will never look away from how much she supports and loves me. If we can help one person, one family, we will achieve our mission. If we are able to help many and spread this message of positivity and hope worldwide, we can change the lives of KGs everywhere.

MARCI

I discuss in my own story, that my biological father was Level Three Batshit Krazy. I attribute my own quick flaring, jump-out-the-window style of temper to him, even though I never met the man. No one on my mom's side acts like this, so I imagine it must be a *nature trait* that I inherited from my PsychoDad, along with my awkward cocked eyebrow. From my mother, I can trace OCD, the need for control, some degree of grandiosity, and my cankles. I can also trace my intelligence, work ethic, generosity and dedication to education and a better life directly to my mother, my maternal grandmother Mollie, and my great-grandmother Dora. I am descended on that side from highly determined and traumatized Russian Jews who immigrated to America in search of religious freedom and a better life. Hard work and placing a high value on education were intentionally cultivated positive traits that led to success through my maternal family line.

As my family dynamics roll downhill, Courtney also has a high degree of intelligence, a strong work ethic, cankles (less pronounced than mine, thank God), and OCD traits that were likely compounded by similar challenges on her father's side. Her particular flavor of Krazy is more of an internalized type like her father's, which means that instead of needing to control her environment like I do, she becomes perfectionistic and over-controls herself. She, and I, have both been Batshit Level Three Krazy in our past, but through a lot of hard work, have probably evolved to Level One. This is the business of my family that plays out in a myriad of ways, shapes and forms, for better and for worse.

If I had been more self-aware of my own unfinished family business and had done more work on myself earlier in my life, would Courtney's mental health challenges have been any different? I think that the answer to this is, unfortunately, yes. I never told my kids anything about my own Krazy past, thinking that I was sparing them the environmental influence of that information during their young and formative years. Now, in retrospect, I believe I was wrong. If I had been more forthcoming about my own life experiences and challenges, it might have somewhat altered the course for Courtney. I can see how much of my own unfinished business was unknowingly passed down to her.

Understanding nature and nurture, parts, individuating the True Self, and intentional awareness of FABs goes a long way in creating a healthier self and family. Awareness and ownership are the first necessary steps for intentional change. Then comes the hard work of implementing that in our lives patiently and lovingly over time. One of the best things we can do for ourselves, our children, and for future generations, is to take care of as much of our unfinished family business, as soon as we can.

CHAPTER 8

Relapse is a Part of Recovery

"I've seen the needle and the damage done. A little part of it in everyone, but every junkies like a setting sun . . . "
—Neil Young

"Try, try, try to understand . . . He's a magic man."
—Heart

MARCI

Sometimes people experience a rare *aha moment*, and that life-changing experience becomes the catalyst for real and lasting change. An example of this is a near death experience. There is a distinct before and after period, and things are never the same afterwards. Change may come easily after the event, and there is often no turning back to the previous life. I have a dear friend who experienced such a change after waking up from an eight-month-long coma. Her life of debauchery was effortlessly behind her when she woke up, and the light of God has miraculously shone through her eyes ever since. This is nothing short of inspiring to behold. But most of the time, change does not happen so efficiently.

Usually, we become aware of something in our life that is not working for us through repeated patterns of painful experiences that I refer to as "messages from the universe." Over time we may choose to embrace change, but only because the pain of staying the same became worse than the pain of changing. Through careful cultivation and tending to new thoughts or behaviors, like a struggling houseplant, this fledgling aspect of the self can grow roots. Over time this germinates a new element of the self, which, if reinforced, becomes a new normal. This process involves tremendous fortitude. I marvel at this because as far as I know, human beings are the only species that can do it. We have the ability to consciously change and direct our evolution for the betterment of ourselves, our loved ones, and for future generations.

Here is an example. Although I don't like to admit this, I used to be a smoker. I started smoking in the junior high bathroom when I was fourteen to hang out with the cool kids. Of course, I became addicted. I attempted to quit many times over the years but was not successful until I had my first child at age thirty-six. I did quit during my pregnancy, but immediately returned as soon as I had her. Embarrassingly, as a new mom, I would put her in the bouncy seat and rush outside for a smoke. I would take a few drags, get dizzy since I was not used to the smoke, rush inside full of guilt, wash up so I did not smell like smoke, and hate myself. The pain of staying the same eventually reached its threshold. I was able to quit at that moment and never look back.

Another example of lasting change is when Courtney hit rock bottom with her depression. At age eighteen, after suffering from anxiety and suicidal depression for more than five years, Courtney had to medically withdraw from her first semester at her dream college. This was a low point for all of us. I will never forget packing up her beautiful single dorm room overlooking the Hudson River and heading home to face yet another treatment program. As she was now eighteen, this time she attended not as an adolescent, but in an adult program where she was by far the youngest patient. She was a mess of self-loathing, humiliation, and pain. She had been back home for a few days and we were sitting on the couch together. She looked me squarely in the eye and boldly said, "I am done living this way. I will not be fifty still fighting this horrible depression because it will kill me. I have to beat this." And so she did. I have never seen her put her mind to anything the way she did that fall and winter. Her deep pain and fierce determination to change were the catalysts that allowed her to take her life back and to start to grow into the person she is today. Not that this was without severe challenges or free of relapse episodes, because that is the reality of living with mental illness. But even that was the start of her path forward. This is the process of recovery and relapse and what all self-directed, internally driven change involves.

What is a Relapse?

The basic definition of a relapse is the return of troubling symptoms or behaviors after a period of wellness or abstinence. It is the deterioration of a state of health or balance after there has been some improvement. This is also known by other names or terms including recidivism, a slip, *oh shit it's back*, or *oops I did it again*. Relapse is a normal process and occurs so frequently that it is considered part of the mental health and addiction recovery process. This is why the title of this chapter is "Relapse is a Part of Recovery."

Although relapse often relates to addiction, the same dynamics hold true with mental health challenges. Three aspects of relapse are helpful to consider, especially when the goal is prevention. These include Emotional Relapse, Mental Relapse and Physical Relapse. The earlier on in the process a relapse can be prevented, the better chance for a positive outcome.

Emotional Relapse

This type of relapse is often the first indicator that a relapse is on the horizon. Emotions become increasingly negative, and moodiness, anger, and irritability intensify. Other emotional signs of unbalance may also present, including anxiety, sadness, sleep or appetite disturbance, and withdrawal from support systems. This should be considered a yellow warning light—trouble is likely brewing.

Mental Relapse

Thinking or obsessing about relapse indicates a mental relapse. Old coping strategies become increasingly attractive. Cravings, planning and bargaining (which will be discussed in greater detail below) intensify. This is a red light; if intervention does not occur, it is probably a matter of time until a physical relapse occurs.

Physical Relapse

A return to old behaviors is called physical relapse. This can involve cutting, using substances, or disappearing from work or school and retreating to bed.

A full-blown relapse is incredibly painful for the person who suffers, as well as for their loved ones. At its worst, relapse can have deadly consequences; in a best-case scenario, significant knowledge and helpful information can come from the experience. The natural tendency for people who have suffered through challenging conditions is to retreat into a honeymoon period. No one wants to think about relapse, especially early on in the recovery process. This type of resistance or denial is natural, but is not helpful for sustainable, long-term recovery. Like the stock market, it's better to have a plan in place to deal with the inevitable ups and downs. It is an ineffective strategy to be reactive to the fluctuations that will surely occur along the way. This is why it is so important to think about relapse prevention as early on in the recovery process as possible.

Preventing Relapse

Avoiding and preventing mental health and addiction relapses have some main aspects that are important to understand. These include awareness of thought, behavior, and biological patterns; understanding triggers and warning signs; committing to change; enlisting proper support; and creating resilience. When we understand and plan for these elements, the risk of relapse can be greatly reduced. The earlier a small slide is intercepted, the less of a chance it has of becoming a lager slip, a painful fall, or a full-blown crisis.

Pattern Awareness

Identifying the thinking and behavior patterns that supported mental illness or addiction is an important part of reworking those patterns and rewiring the brain. Healthy habits must be created and supported over time to allow for sustained change. There is a cause and effect nature to human patterns, and usually we can see the warning signs of relapse long before it occurs.

The same behavioral and biological processes play out with any conditioned or addictive process, whether it involves relationships, substances, workaholism, sex addiction, sugar, shopping, or gambling. Anything that activates the chemical dopamine in the brain creates a neural pathway in the brain, whether created by pleasure or pain. Dopamine is one of the three neurotransmitters that are most responsible for mood, emotion, and thinking. These neurochemicals are incredibly powerful, and it is important to be mindful of the strong influence they hold over us. It is easy to become dependent on, or addicted to, this intense chemical response, whether the cascade comes from the experience of love, pain, or eating cheese. Balanced and stable living produces a much less intense chemical response. Therefore, effectively rewiring the brain depends on becoming acclimated to the new subtlety of different brain chemistry.

Triggers and Warning Signs

Those who have been through recovery and relapse share that there are usually clear warning signs prior to a relapse. Emotional and mental relapse often comes before a physical relapse, even if it seemed to come out of nowhere. Triggers, which are specific events that affect our emotional state, can set off a chain reaction that leads to conditioned behavior patterns. Cravings must be anticipated and dealt with. Becoming aware of the triggers and warning signs that precede a relapse is a vital part of prevention.

H.A.L.T.

Twelve-step programs use simple slogans that are helpful and effective to promote pattern awareness. The acronym HALT is a great example. Beware of becoming too **Hungry, Angry, Lonely** or **Tired**, as these factors can make us vulnerable. *Stinking thinking* (aka emotional or mental relapse), left unchecked, is a slippery slope that can result in a relapse. *One day at a time* reminds us to stay present and deal with what is in front of us. Tuning into the triggers and warning signs that set off emotional, mental, and physical patterns is effective in redirecting old behavioral patterns. Proactive planning can help us "cope ahead" in stressful situations.

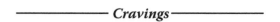

Cravings

Craving substances or old behaviors used for pleasure or coping are common, especially shortly after discontinuing use. As we have discussed, pleasurable behaviors release the neurochemical dopamine, but so do behaviors that create pain, such as cutting. The established patterns that connect emotions and behaviors are hard to change. This is why anticipating cravings and having plans in place to cope and redirect is a major part of any relapse prevention plan. If my favorite cigarette of the day comes after a meal, planning for that and scheduling a walk instead is a great way to deal with that craving. If I used to cut when I was angry, I am likely to crave that behavior for a long time after I stop doing it. Keep in mind that a craving may pass quickly, unless it is reinforced by engaging the behavior. The longer I redirect my cravings and create new thinking and behavior patterns, the less frequent and intense cravings become over time.

———— *Mentally Rehearsing and Bargaining* ————

Thinking or reminiscing about old behaviors is a sign that recovery is on shaky ground. The more we indulge thoughts of relapse, the more likely it is to occur. Bargaining means telling ourselves it is OK if we use just once or at some point in the future, which paves the way for a relapse. If we begin to mentally rehearse or bargain with ourselves about old behaviors, this is essentially the same thing as a mental relapse and is considered a very high-risk situation. The longer this thinking process occurs without redirection, the more likely a relapse will occur. This is why using coping skills, employing support, and committing to change over time is so important.

Commitment to Change

Once unhealthy patterns are established, it is incredible how much effort and energy is actually required to change their course. Strong brain chemicals create neurological pathways that only get more deeply ingrained when reinforced over time, through repeated experiences. Creating new pathways is not a simple process. A strong appetite for change and real dedication is necessary to create these new thought processes and behaviors. Eventually, this commitment to change will carve out new neurological pathways which become the more intentional patterns we wish to cultivate. Think of this process like unwanted water that seeps into a basement. Every time it rains the water flows in faster, because the grooves in the ground are deeper. To correct the problem, the existing pathways must be redirected, and the structure itself needs to be sealed up. Next time it rains, the water can start to follow the new pathways, and the old, but now sealed, cracks in the foundation will help to keep the basement dry.

Change is an intentional process that takes energy and effort. Increasing and maintaining our focus on the reasons why we want to change, including the benefits and consequences of not changing, helps to carve out the new grooves that will promote and maintain recovery. Change is hard. We must develop, reinforce, and commit again and again to the change we seek, in order to build the new pathways and habits which will support a new lifestyle.

Finding Support

Meaningful support can involve many things: self-care, therapy, medicine, family or community assistance, church or spiritual connection. Support can include anything that envelopes an individual in the love and safety of community. None of us are islands unto ourselves. New recovery benefits from as much support as possible. The more the better, from as many sources as possible. There is no such thing as too much support.

The twelve-step model is nothing short of brilliant for support. In a best-case scenario it would look like this: A newly sober individual is strongly encouraged to attend ninety meetings in ninety days. This is the beginning of their new circle of community support. They are also advised to obtain a same-sex sponsor to show them the ropes, and to begin to work on a program of recovery. Their family members and significant others are advised to attend Al Anon meetings to deal with their own challenges and learn about proper support without enabling. The singular focus of the first ninety days is to build a strong base of individual, community, and family support. The longer and deeper the support the better the outcome is, which is vitally important to prevent future relapses.

Creating Resilience

Resilience is the ability to effectively deal with our challenges and bounce back from adversity. Building and strengthening resilience is one of the most important ways to bulletproof recovery. Developing good coping skills and committing to a meaningful self-care routine are some of the most helpful ways to ward off relapse and cement a fulfilling and balanced lifestyle. Any time we go through challenging life experiences and grow stronger, we promote confidence, inner strength, and resilience. The more we can cope with our challenges and handle stress, the better for long-term recovery.

An Episode Versus a Crisis

It is important to understand the difference between an episode and a crisis. An episode is considered an event or series of events that occur during a specific timeframe. From a mental health standpoint, an episode usually involves some degree of imbalance. For example, a depressive episode means that there is a period where depression has presented itself. A panic attack is considered an intense episode of anxiety. An episode is quite different from a crisis, which refers to a time of intense challenge or difficulty. For example, an untreated episode of depression under certain conditions can progress into a crisis. Sad mood and lack of motivation, typical of episodic symptoms, can intensify into sleep disturbance, loss of appetite, and even psychosis or a suicide attempt. A crisis can be dangerous or even deadly and must be managed properly to avoid a disaster. The best way to prevent a crisis is to identify and deal effectively with an episode.

There is no straight line forward when it comes to wellness. There will be episodes to contend with along the way, this is for sure. An episode can lead to a crisis if not properly dealt with, and managing a crisis has high stakes, which are best avoided whenever possible. But an episode properly managed can resolve fairly quickly, and life can return to normal. An example of this can be found with Seasonal Affective Disorder (SAD). People who suffer from SAD will predictably have some type of increased anxiety or hypomanic tendencies to some degree each spring. Most will also experience an episode of depression in the fall. Misunderstood, this can have a huge effect on individuals and their families, even leading to the need for a higher level of care or hospitalization. However, if SAD is properly understood and managed well, there may be a bit of a bump in the road, or little effect at all. The happy lightbox[14] goes on or off as daylight savings time changes season, and the wheel of life continues on, helped by tweaking meds, utilizing hard learned tools and skills, and/or having an understanding and supportive family. Therefore it is so important to understand the difference between an episode and a crisis, and to be able to respond accordingly.

Providing Support Without Enabling

Support without enabling is nothing short of an art form. Understanding the differences requires a little or a lot of education, depending on where we are in our own evolutionary process. Based on our own, highly personal vision of love and parenting styles, the concept of support versus enabling can be murky at best.

Here is an example. I became a mother at a time when attachment parenting was all the rage. The premise was that if you fill your child's cup to the top with constant love and attention, they will go into the world safe and secure. According to the highly popular *Mothering* magazine, the family bed should be available for as long as mutually desired, and babywearing in slings and ridiculously expensive Baby Bjorn front packs was highly encouraged. The more physical and emotional connection between child and mother for the longest amount of time possible, was thought to be best for secure child

---

14   full spectrum light therapy can be very helpful for seasonal affective disorder.

development. I bought into this philosophy hook, line, and sinker. We now understand, that this can actually foster dependency and, according to some experts, contribute to love addiction.

I have come to realize that despite my best intentions, Courtney slept in my bed for way too long, and when she became mentally ill, we became joined at the hip. It took me many rounds of parent DBT training to understand that in many ways, I was reinforcing many of Courtney's unhealthy behaviors. Because of my own poor boundaries and mitigating her dealing with natural consequences, she did not develop the internal controls that were necessary to deal with her own life challenges until much later. Unwittingly, I contributed to a poor outcome until I learned better.

Boundaries are an important part of being supportive without enabling. We must respect the lines between what is OK and what is not OK, for ourselves and others, based on our values and needs. If I am being asked to do something that is not comfortable for me, I need to take some time and think about my course of action. Crossing lines, or pushing boundaries, is often involved in enabling scenarios. This can be a difficult subject to deal with and not easy to understand. There is a lot of information available about the important topic of boundaries, and I encourage you to dig deeper into this subject if warranted.

Each of us must be open to our individual and family dynamics. Awareness of how this interplay manifests with our loved ones is a key part of being helpful. The last thing we want to do is unwittingly sabotage a fragile recovery process. Learning the difference between healthy support versus enabling is a key factor in preventing relapse. This is why groups such as Al Anon, Codependents Anonymous, or quality family therapy are so important for sustained recovery. We all need to be a part of the solution, and not reinforce, or be a part of the problem, as much as we possibly can.

COURTNEY

Do you ever feel like you are taking one step forward and two steps back? It seems like sometimes we're making great progress toward something, whether it be a goal, an accomplishment, or anything else going on in our daily lives, and that progress can turn around very quickly when we face a major setback. For many years, throughout my journey through KrazyLand, this has been a pattern for me. As far as I would get with my mental health, I would hit a low point, give into old habits, and go through relapse again. Relapse is something that many of us face. Nobody wants to think about relapsing. We want to think positively most of the time, and keeping that attitude is not a problem. But when the unfortunate situation of relapsing occurs, what is most important is that we learn from our mistakes, and do everything in our power to not give in again.

I'm currently in recovery for my self-destructive pattern of self-harming when things get really rough in my life. I had gone two years without self-harming, and then I did it again. Similarly, at one point I did not give in to my compulsion of (triple) checking the lights in my room for a month, and then one day, I gave in, and relapsed by engaging in these checking patterns to satisfy my OCD. Although the saying "one step forward, two steps back" can *feel* relatable for many, most of the time, in reality, it's "two steps forward, one step back." Most of the time (not including episodes of mania, depression, or something similar), we are progressing through life taking many steps forward to meet our goals. However, throughout the course of our daily lives, we face many difficult emotions in our Krazy brains. Although we work to be our best selves and not regress, it has absolutely proven true in my life that relapse is a part of recovery.

There are many types of relapse. Some types include relapsing with emotions, self-harm, alcohol, or drugs, relapsing with OCD symptoms, bad relationship choices, issues with food, or any other thought process or behavior that is unhealthy for us. In my experience, relapse occurs when we cannot take any more of a situation. After resisting a "stress-relieving" (not in a positive way) activity or behavior for a while, we give in and do it. Relapse can, of course, happen, even if we have not participated in the destructive behavior for a long period of time. Sometimes we relapse because we cannot take the stressors in our lives anymore, but this can also be true if we cannot take the stress of our hectic, Krazy brains. So, both situational and emotional problems can cause a relapse.

Relapse can be really, really tough, and I know this from the experience of relapsing with self-harm, eating disorder thoughts/behaviors, unhealthy relationships, and OCD symptoms. I have learned a lot from these relapses, and they have helped me to get to know myself better and be more stable and happy, but at what cost? Although it may seem like it is the end of the world and that you must restart your recovery from the beginning, you can also treat it as an opportunity to give it your best shot. This can help us feel more empowered and in control of our life. This experience can give you the strength you need to push through a tough time in the future.

Relapse can lead us toward strength and wisdom. But it can also lead to deadly consequences. Although this may sound strange and distorted, it can be comforting to turn to something that has helped to calm stressors previously. This is where it is important to recognize, and really accept, which behaviors are helpful and which ones are harmful for our physical and mental state. For example, although self-harm has been a technique that I have used to try and feel better in the past, it is now very clear to me that this is **not** a strategy I should use to cope with difficult emotions. Not only is it dangerous, it does not help me feel better. It actually causes guilt and remorse. It does more way more harm for me than good. The same thing goes for relapsing with eating disorder thoughts and behaviors, relapsing with chemical addiction, or going back to a destructive and toxic relationship. Giving in to these old behaviors may seem to help, but does much more damage than good and may actually be harmful or even fatal. I try to stop and think before impulsively giving into old coping habits and ask myself if this behavior will help or hurt my mental and physical state in the long run. Although short-term gratification can sometimes feel like the best route, we have to think of our wellbeing in the long term. We have to consider how our actions have an effect on the way we think and feel, particularly about ourselves. Oftentimes, if we relapse, we feel a great sense of guilt and remorse after giving into the behavior. If we prevent it in the first place, using all of our skills and power to tough through the hard times, we will not have to face these feelings.

Over the years, I have learned an important lesson. If I surround myself with positive influences and people who bring me more joy than stress, I tend to be a happier and more level person. The more drama and bullshit that goes on in our lives, the more we need an escape or a coping mechanism. The more we experience negative emotions, the more we have to work to keep ourselves happy. The more we are stressed, the more we have to think positive thoughts and allow ourselves to feel calm and not frantic. The more we are sad, the more we have to look at cute pictures of dogs and inspiring quotes on the internet to put a smile on our faces. I have made it a point to be around people who support me, try to understand what I am going through, and listen with an open heart and open mind. This has made a huge difference in how I cope with my pain. Instead of keeping my emotions bottled up, I talk about what is going on with people who I love and trust.

Relapse occurs when we cannot tolerate the way that we are feeling anymore, so we give into a bad habit to *try* to feel better. It is really hard not to give in and use the substance "just this once," or "just skip this one meal." But it is really important to remember that using positive coping skills are truly better for us and will cause much less remorse, damage, and pain. I have always disliked when people (mostly my family members) turn to me during an argument or time when I am heated and tell me to use my DBT skills.[15] I use these skills anyway, because I know that they help me feel better without causing more damage, and this has saved me from relapsing on many occasions. However, in a moment of extreme distress, it

---

15   *DBT=Dialectical Behavioral Therapy: A type of therapy used to help people who are struggling with mental illness which helps them to calm down in times of severe distress (which I have been practicing for the last four years).*

bothers me when others try and tell me what could help me feel better. I know from experience that it is important to develop a set of skills to have in your pocket when you are in an episode, having a bad day, or just need to turn around your mood. After attaining these skills, it is up to us to use these tools when we most need them.

It is important to stay dedicated to your wellness and to mentally decide not to give up when life gets difficult and unbearable. If you have anything less than pure dedication to yourself, it will be really hard to stop yourself from succumbing to old coping mechanisms that are not good for you. Whether it is joining a group to learn skills to cope with mental illness (like DBT) or deciding to go to therapy, as long as you are doing something to better yourself and challenge yourself, then you are on the track to preventing relapse. If you are not participating in activities that will help your mental state, and you are struggling with your emotions or behaviors, then you might want to ask yourself what is really holding you back. Even incorporating ten minutes of yoga and/or meditation into the day can help you to begin to live harmoniously with your thoughts and emotions. Exercising in any form, participating in self-care, taking a walk in nature, or doing anything that gives you time to feel good and happy, can help stabilize your mood and cope with stress. Therapy and groups are also great to talk about what we are going through and learn skills and get feedback. You are not alone!

Going through pain over and over is not only frustrating but also sad. Feeling like you have failed yourself is a crappy feeling. There is no good way to put it or sugarcoat the truth about this. Relapse is a part of recovery. But does it have to be?!? Maybe, maybe not. KGs, please be as tough as you can for yourself now, and over the course of time, things will usually get easier. I would love to say that things definitely get easier, and they very well might, but everyone is going to face bumps in the road. Learning how to cope is the most important part of making relapse a thing of the past. When I look down at the scars on my body, I sometimes wonder if I am going to be forty-five or eighty-five and experience another relapse. I like to think that I am strong enough not give in to the impulses I have, but I have said that before about the same things. So, for now, I will use all the skills in the world, surround myself with positive and supportive individuals, remember the things that my amazing mental health professionals have taught me, and think back to the wise words of my parents and loved ones: This, too, shall pass. Relapse does not mean we are starting over, but it may mean that we need to work harder to be happy and control our Krazy brains. We must be strong to prevent relapse.

MARCI

I am an eternal optimist. I see the glass as half full, I look at painful experiences as growth opportunities, and I usually wake up happy and ready to greet the day. I am also an *Outie,* in belly button language, rather than an *Innie,* meaning I externalize my emotions rather than internalize them. How then, does this relate to relapse? All humans have a default neurologic style—we tend to fight, run away, or freeze when faced with extreme stress. My personality and worldview make me a fighter. I am Marci from Canarsie: I will come out slugging rather than lay down. Courtney has an entirely different personality and makeup. She's an Innie. She freezes and shuts down. She bears her pain inside rather than spread it around. Internalizing takes a different toll on the soul than externalizing does, which can lead to OCD, depression, or addiction. Please keep in mind that I am not an addictions specialist; I will leave that to Eric, Steve, and the other experts in this chapter who are. But I deeply wish that Courtney would scream, yell, or cry rather than hurt herself trying to deal with her pain, any day of the week.

Reading over Courtney's section, I am struck by her level of understanding about what relapse means in her own short life—a maladaptive attempt to cope with painful and overwhelming thoughts and feelings. Sadly, these tracks of pain were laid down way too early for her and were reinforced throughout the years she kept these events, emotions, and responses to herself. My heart breaks for what she has been through, and as a mom I have a long way to go in coming to grips with all that has happened.

I also know as a professional, the longer and more frequently a thought or behavior occurs, the more deeply ingrained it becomes. The same holds true in rewiring our patterns—the more frequently healthier patterns occur over time, the more they will also become a new normal. But the younger the tracks of trauma and maladaptive coping patterns are laid down the worse the prognosis is, because "the clay is not yet dry," so to speak. Like a tree that grew around an impediment during the growth cycle, it will likely be to some degree forever altered. Similarly, the earlier emotional issues are identified and treated, the better the outcome is likely to be. I am grateful for the knowledge that exists regarding relapse and recovery, and especially so for the experts that share their vast experience with us here.

EXPERT ADVICE

To give greater clarification and context to this very important topic of relapse, we turned to two of the most trusted and reputable experts available in the field of relapse and recovery. Our sincere gratitude goes out to Eric Kispert and Steven Donohue for their valuable advice.

Eric Kispert, LCSW, an expert we heard from in Chapter Six, has been a licensed clinical social worker for over twenty-five years. His knowledge and expertise is vast, as is his humanity and compassion. I feel lucky to call Eric my trusted mentor and friend.

> *I like to look at relapse from the standpoint of the relational cycle: harmony, disharmony (another word for that is relapse) and repair, to move into a deeper place of harmony.*

Whether we are talking about our mental wellness and some deviation from that mental wellness (relapse), or addiction, or a marriage or other relationship, or Bipolar disorder, I think that there are a lot of similarities between all of them regarding wellness and relapse. Ideally, when we are in wellness/recovery mode and all is going well, our Life Recovery (see below), including the emotional, spiritual, relational, and physical aspects of our lives are going well and are in balance. When we are not moving forward in these areas, this can be considered a relapse.

Relapse can be a bit of a sting word, because it suggests an all or nothing mentality. It may be more helpful to think of this in terms of 'there is a part of me that just does not have the wherewithal to keep moving forward, that is hitting a pause button, is moving sideways or regressing in my life recovery balance.' It is important to keep in mind, especially for the loved ones of someone who for example stopped taking their Bipolar medicine and wound up in the hospital, that this does not mean that there was a relapse of the entire person. But rather this wedge or part of the person went sideways. When I work with people who are in recovery from addiction, in AA language for example, if you have a year sober and you have a month relapse, and then you have a month sober, you are considered to be sober for a month. If I am bipolar and I have a year of solid and sustained mental sustained wellness, and then I go off my meds for a month and I act crazy, and then I am back on my meds for a month, I like to say that I have a year and a month of wellness under my belt. All the good work I did does not get undone because I had a setback. I like to look at the entirety of the time and effort a person put into a concerted effort into recovery—with a very broad definition of Life Recovery. Over time, in a myriad of areas, there has been much positive. Often with relapse, especially for the family and loved ones of those affected, the good work that preceded the relapse may become eclipsed. I like to look at the full picture of the efforts and growth achieved, and that is why the term relapse can become polarizing. It makes the notion of going through the cycle of harmony, disharmony, and repair so helpful to keep in mind, because when we can look at the totality of progress there will be less to repair along the way. Don't throw the baby out with the bathwater.

A term I started using years ago is Life Recovery, partly because it destigmatizes and mitigates the shame that is often associated with mental illness and addiction. When I am in Life Recovery, I am not looking at this through a monolithic lens of "I am Bipolar and I am either doing well or I am doing poorly." Rather, I look at my wellness through the lens of "I am a citizen of my community, I am a member of a family, an employee or employer, I have a myriad of areas in my life and body," and I look at my wellness through the lens of all of these areas. When I start to make a commitment towards improvement in all of these areas, this is my Life Recovery. I came to this path through dealing with my alcoholism, then I realized I have work to do with my frustration tolerance, so I began to work on my anger management. And then the longer I was sober and the broader the lens of my recovery, I realized I had to take charge of my DNA and the propensity in my family toward morbid obesity, so I began to integrate another area of life wellness into my recovery. Then I realized my spirituality also needed to come into play. Looking at this as taking steps of recovery rather than a series of relapses and working on ownership of all areas of my life, is Life Recovery. Taking steps toward a whole, fully actualized self has many aspects involved. Areas of wellness to consider may include self-inquiry around what improvements need to be made in these following areas:

Mental: *Our neuro-biological wellness (this includes all mental health diagnoses).*

Physical: *What am I doing to take care of my body/temple including self-harming behaviors, nicotine, a healthy relationship with food, consumption of or dependence on substances?*

Spiritual: *How present, intact or robust is my relationship with the universe or the Divine?*

Relational: *How healthy are my boundaries, how are my connections, how is my self-esteem or my grandiosity, am I in the Center of Health? (Terry Real RLT).*

Avocation/Career: *My sustenance, my relationship with the material world, contributions and satisfaction through my working life.*

Quoting a beloved friend of mine, Father Martin, (and I use this line a lot . . .) 'Where there is life, there is hope.' A dear friend of mine shared with me in the last month of his life, 'Eric, there are two things that are most important to life, hope and appetite. If you lose either one, you will lose your life.' And he is right, if you lose either one it is all over. Sadly, the facts are that the majority of people do not sustain recovery for over five years. We have to have an appetite for wellness, a desire, grit, determination, and a willingness to change. Without an appetite for life, we stay stuck in relapse and we never transcend or find our way back to healthy. Most of those who do not achieve long term sobriety or recovery do not have the appetite for recovery; and then the hope dwindles, and then their life dwindles.

Steven Donohue,who we have also heard from in the chapter on relationships, is an Iraqi war veteran, a social worker, a life coach, and entrepreneur. His real talk and practical advice is both valuable and accessible.

Relapse is a powerful word. Some words have too much power; this is one of them. The power of the word derives more from the stigma surrounding the word than the word itself. Before we dive too far into relapse and its impact on us and our lives, it must first be defined.

Ask anyone you can find on the street. I believe you'd see that a person will associate a relapse with addiction. I don't blame these people; the only relapse that society commonly recognizes is addiction.

But why? There must be a connection that can be built between addiction and relapse as it genuinely exists in context. Although both a verb and a noun, relapse is operationally defined as 'the deterioration of one's mental state after a period of improvement.' When speaking about how to define a word such as relapse, it is essential to understand its nuances. Breaking it down a bit, the phrasing of 'deterioration' and 'period of improvement' are key identifiers to understand further what relapse is. To identify a relapse, first, you must determine that there's been something to relapse from in the first place.

For example, if a person is suffering from recurrent panic attacks due to past trauma, they have been in treatment, and the attacks stop. Fast forward three months, the attacks begin to occur again. The panic attack reoccurring is a relapse. The second identified phrasing of a relapse is the period of improvement aspect. An example of this improvement from the above example is that the therapy effectively halted the panic attacks for the three months.

In my experience of behavioral health and addiction, there are elements that all relapses have in common: the thought, the urge, the relapse, and the recovery.

Thoughts and urges may not seem that common when discussing mental illness, but they are very relevant. The relevance of thought is in the mind that the person experiences. Suppose a person who is combatting a mental illness begins to have fleeting thoughts that become more consistent. In that case, the thought can begin to develop into a form of obsession, similar to a person beginning to feel anxiety levels increasing. Over time, those thoughts can manifest into a physical or intense mental urge. Once the urge sets in, there are only two ways to respond; either they will have a relapse or cope effectively.

Whether a relapse occurs, or positive coping mechanisms are engaged, both provide a recovery level after the decision. If the choice is to relapse, the person will generally experience instant, decreased anxiety, and emotion. This does not negate the strong potential for feelings of guilt, shame, or a recurrence in the negative feelings that came before the relapse. If a person decides to utilize a positive coping mechanism (i.e., deep breathing technique), they will experience decreased anxiety levels.

In my past, clients reported to me that the relapse released the tension much more than the preferred coping mechanism. I found this to be astonishing at the time. Still, over time, I learned more, and it is the immediate release that they were seeking, not necessarily the behavior that the relapse represented. We often get very held up on the relapse itself and not the behavior leading up to or the representation of a relapse.

Coping with Relapse

How does one cope with a relapse? To answer this question, I find it pivotal to look at multiple perspectives. Starting with the person who experienced the relapse, we can learn that the relapse to them is a very personal and vulnerable experience. Quite often, the person who has experienced the relapse feels negative about the relapse and will begin to seek external support. Although it may not seem true in the beginning, loving and supporting the person is truly what they want, not the action of a relapse. Looking at relapse as it stands, it is a person's deterioration. How does one find positives in the deterioration of behavior or period they have worked so diligently to avoid?

If you are the person who is experiencing the relapse, you don't have to tear yourself down any further.

Below are three tips to immediately commit to once a relapse occurs:

1. *Tell someone. Your honesty and transparency will reaffirm and maintain the continuity of your treatment or effort to change the behavior.*
2. *Evaluate the situation. Quite often, you'll see where there was a break in positive behavior, and there you'll find your lesson to be learned.*
3. *Accept it. Taking accountability for your actions, and recognizing the relapse as something that has happened, is a positive approach to preventing it from becoming something that happens.*

What do you do when someone you love dearly experiences a relapse?

Is it easy to watch someone that you love deteriorate? No, of course not, but if one in five people in the United States has a mental illness, is it that far-fetched to believe that the families must understand and cope with relapse as well?

The family experience is a bit harder to understand than the individual relapsing. One of the critical reasons for this difficulty is that the person relapsing presents a sense of control over the situation. In contrast, the family members have little to no control over the relapsed person's behavior.

In reality, the family has a tremendous amount of control over the situation they are involved in. Unfortunately, it just isn't going to change the fact that a relapse occurred, but the control is in the response, not the reaction. In context, the reaction is the initial emotional response triggered by the reception of information, in this case, the relapse. The response is the action that occurs upon the discovery of the relapse.

Breaking this down a bit further, families take on more responsibility than they intend to at times. Our familial constructs take over, presenting the opportunity to latch onto our own and shower our loved ones with love and compassion, for some. Another common thread is when the family completely removes itself from the relapsed person's life. Which way is right? Which way is wrong? That is a question that can't be answered entirely by any expert, therapist, guru, or coach. It is a personal choice that falls on the shoulders of those never prepared for the weight it bears.

Too often, the family finds itself feeling a sense of suffering while coincidentally feeling a sense of empowerment when rallying around their loved one. The suffering is anchored in fear of the unknown (i.e., death), and empowerment is anchored in faith (i.e., life). Above all, it is integral not to have high expectations of either party (relapsed person or family) but to identify what is within each party's control and establish boundaries.

One of the most challenging discussions to have with families experiencing relapse is the concept of enabling. In my experience, discussing the idea of enabling the person in relapse with families often takes more than one session to establish a firm understanding. The more I talked about the topic, the more enraged I could see the family getting. They began to project their anger toward themselves onto me for bringing the subject up. Over time, we were able to come to an understanding that I was only providing insight. However, the more significant outcome was the family's realization that they were enabling their beloved family member.

To clear the air, we all enable people. It's life. Sometimes it has negative consequences. You can love and support your loved one without enabling for periods of time. The work is in continued maintenance. I encourage you to use this book as a tool and guide in moments of weakness and strength.

How does a person support without enabling?

I am going to keep it simple in a three-step process.

1. ***Establish boundaries and enforce them.*** *One of the quickest ways to enable a person is to not hold them accountable, even more so if boundaries have previously been established.*

2. ***Identify what is in your control*** *and allow the rest to fall into place. Although it sounds like an actionable step, a significant majority is emotional respect for your boundaries and threshold.*

3. ***Trust the process.*** *Too often, when we are engaged with loved ones combating hardships, we innately want to step in and be there. In theory, this makes a lot of sense, but in reality, it can adversely affect a person's development, both the relapsed person and the family.*

If you're a family member of a person experiencing a relapse, below are three tips for you to utilize in times of need:

1. ***Don't blame yourself:*** *as we grow in life, so does our responsibility and accountability level. Ownership of our actions must fall on ourselves.*

2. ***Talk.*** *There is no shortage of support groups and professionals to speak to. Going at it alone may seem to be the right thing for various reasons (i.e., culture, money, and shame), but guidance is essential.*

3. ***Live.*** *Easier said than done, but the importance of continuing to live your life is a crucial element when coping with a relapse of a loved one. The preservation of yourself creates a more stable environment. Remember, you can't give CPR without air to share.*

In closing, I'd like to say that whether you have experienced relapse directly or indirectly, it affects everyone. Even hearing that a person relapsed can be drastically impactful. Be at peace with what the universe provides, as it will always provide you with opportunity, which alone is peaceful.

The Long Road Home: Hope and a New Normal

The perseverance and dedication that is necessary for change to occur is nothing short of miraculous. The strength of character and desire for a better life in the midst of our hardest times is the most inspiring form of the human spirit. Although the process of recovery is hard, relapse is even harder. We must be resilient and hold a vision of what life can look like when our hard work and dedication pays off. Hope breaks the bondage of adherence to the legacy of suffering.

We step forward, fall down, get up, lean on our support systems and loved ones, dig deep inside, and step forward again. And again. This is the creation of a new normal and the beginning of our long road home. The process is no less intense than tectonic plates crashing together to create mountains, or volcanos erupting to make new real estate. A tiny seed takes hold and begins to grow on barren land that eventually becomes a lush forest, capable of supporting amazingly diverse forms of life.

The potential born from the pain of change creates opportunities for growth and liberation of the soul. This is both vulnerability and brazen humanity on full display. As we change and become stronger, we then begin to pave the path forward for others to traverse. We reach out our hand and help those who still struggle and suffer, sharing our hard-earned wisdom and a vision for positive change. To quote another twelve-step slogan, we must give it away to keep it. Welcome to your new home, KGs. And so it is.

PART III

WISDOM, STRENGTH, & HOPE

CHAPTER 9

Wisdom & Strength: Advice from KrazyMamas & Loved Ones

"You've got a friend in me . . . "
—Toy Story

"Lean on me, when you're not strong, and I'll be your friend . . . "
—Bill Withers

Warrior parents and affected loved ones have experienced quite a lot throughout the difficult journey taken alongside our beloved KGs. During our most challenging times, when we are lost or confused, we deeply appreciate the wisdom and strength of others who have been there. Drawing upon their insight and understanding helps us know we are not alone. It illuminates a path forward in the darkness. As we move along through our own process, sharing what we have learned with others helps us to heal and grow. Those who generously chose to share their hard-earned wisdom, provide much needed guidance to those who are suffering. Together, we form a community of support that encircles us all with hope and healing. No one willingly chose to be a member of the KrazyClub, but we are all members now, nonetheless. We must do the best we can with the cards we have been dealt and help each other along the way whenever we can.

Learn, Heal, Teach

There is a saying in the therapy community that instructs us to *"Learn, heal, teach."* In any new situation, and especially during our hardest challenges, we are first in *learn* mode: We are trying to deal with, and make some kind of sense of new information. Once we get our footing and begin to manage what is in front of us, we then have the opportunity to move into *heal* mode. Here, we digest and begin to put our experience into a context or framework, which then becomes part of the story of our lives. At that point, many who have endured significant pain or trauma feel a strong need to *teach.* Becoming an expert on the other side of raging waters helps to give personal meaning to our experiences, connect with others, and provide much needed guidance to the community we have come to belong to. I like to think of this like climbing a steep mountain trail with others. As we move forward on the path, we lend our hand to those behind us who need some help. And when we falter or need support, we reach out our own hand to others who are farther along the trail. Together, we move forward towards the summit.

The origins of the *KrazyGirl (& Guy) Survival Guide* are deeply rooted in the *learn, heal, teach* model. When Courtney was eighteen and starting to get stable after medically withdrawing from her dream college, the idea for this book first came to me. It was my gut instinct that if I could help Courtney transition into *teach* mode, this could assist her in her healing process by planting her on the other side of a long and hard chapter. When I suggested to her that we should write a book together, I felt in my bones that this could not only help the world, it would certainly help us.

Early in the project when we were interviewing experts, I felt immense pride and gratitude for Courtney's participation and collaboration. She was really into the work, and it helped to eclipse her depression. I saw that in itself, as a hopeful sign. As we interviewed her long-time psychiatrist, Dr. Bruce Friedman, her high school psychologist, Ashely DiBiasi, and later her own therapist, Dr. Laura Richardson, I saw Courtney begin to realize that that she could someday join their ranks. I believe this early formation of her new identity was instrumental in her impressive healing and recovery process. As Courtney's strength and confidence grew, she began to build success academically and socially, and her newly forming identity blossomed. As the writing of the *KGPSG* is reaching its conclusion, Courtney is working diligently towards PH. D candidacy in clinical psychology. She is deeply committed to helping others recover from trauma, becoming a college professor, and researching the role of mindfulness practices in mental health and healing. I have one hundred percent confidence that she will achieve and exceed each of her goals, which originated during the darkest of her days. More importantly, *she* believes in this for herself.

In their uncut words, here is a selection of advice generously shared by (mostly) moms, and loved ones who have traveled on this KrazyTrain. Consider what advice feels right for you, and please disregard the rest. We each have an inner truth radar and guidance system that lives deep inside us. Listen to what resonates and feels right for you, because *only you* know what makes sense for your situation. If you have any advice you wish to share with others who are suffering, please contact us, so we can include it in future editions of the Krazy Series.

Our deepest gratitude and respect to all who dug deeply to share their hard-earned knowledge and wisdom, in hopes that it will help others on their journey. Indeed, your wise and insightful words have taught me more than I could have imagined. KrazyMamas—you are true warrior rock stars.

Advice for Parents of Teens

The following advice comes from parents and significant loved ones of teens. You will note that most of this is hands-on and directive. This approach is necessary for effective parenting when our kids are younger and more dependent on us. This is often the time when we first understand that mental illness is present in some way, shape, or form. At the same time we are trying to learn and digest massive amounts of information about diagnosis and treatment options, we are also responsible for managing our child's complicated care. This is an extremely raw and challenging time, and it is common to have a wide range of intense and conflicting emotions.

> **ZG**[16]: *Take it one day at a time, this is a marathon not a sprint. Celebrate the good times even if rare or small! Finally, find a place or support network where you can feel comfortable to talk openly about what you are going through—the warriors need counsel in this battle too! And educate others, so someday talking about mental illness stops being taboo."*

> **MC:** *"Advocate for a 504-plan, IEP, or both. Handle it the way you would a business meeting. Advocate for resources and appropriate documentation. From a home perspective, there are no rules or time limits when it comes to mental illness. Meaning, don't expect your child to be picture-perfect and follow middle, high school, and college the way it is laid out now. There are alternative schools and online schools. Don't put yourself, or your child, on a timetable because the Does down the street are on one."*

---

16   Initials have been used to protect privacy.

MLN: *"Give yourself and your daughter grace. Find an outlet and end hard conversations with, 'I will never give up on you,' or, 'I love you always.' I don't know why this is so important to me, but that's my thing. Last but not least, give a little bit of space if needed. This is the hardest for me."*

KSV: *"My biggest lessons that got me through are:*

1. *Be patient, this is a marathon not a sprint. Maturity plays a role in our children's wellness. They have to learn that treatment, health, and outcomes are all in their hands and control. Until they can take responsibility, it's a long, slow hike carrying them.*

2. *Self-care and taking care of you is essential! Get your own therapist, work on your own beliefs and mental health. If it is exercise, yoga, meditation, or whatever is your thing, make a point to do it.*

3. *You cannot control or change others, you can only control or change how you react and respond to them.*

4. *The kids are listening and appreciate our love and support, even when they are acting out at us. Our words and love will be appreciated when the kids are ready to accept them. Keep trying.*

5. *Medication is not the whole solution. It can be a part of the solution but is never a quick fix. And be patient with meds and changes. You often won't see the full effect of them for weeks or months. And that is extremely frustrating when your kid is in crisis NOW! So the kids (and parents) need other tools and resources to work with the meds.*

6.   *There is a heartbreaking lack of good adolescent psych professionals! Not all therapists, psychiatrists, or psych nurse practitioners are good fits for your child, so keep looking until you find the right person/relationship. You will know it when it happens!"*

SS: *"Seek second, third, or fourth opinions on treatment options, especially if your child has more than one diagnosis."*

BLR: *"An escalated adult cannot de-escalate an escalated child. Walk away, take deep belly breaths, splash cold water on your face. Calm down and then parent, respond, discipline, and redirect."*

MAW: *"Dear KrazyMama: You have just dropped off your child at an inpatient or residential treatment facility for the first time. You are scared, you are worried about your child, you're wondering if you did the right thing. Take a deep breath. Now—this might be the first time that your child has been away from you under the care of professionals. THEY ARE SAFE! Soon, the world will soon explode with transportation issues, visiting and therapist meetings, and someone asking you about background and history—but for now, remember, THEY ARE SAFE! Girl—take a NAP!!"*

ME: *"Not a major revelation, but when they complain or bitch to you about something, they aren't necessarily asking you to fix it. They may just need someone to listen."*

ES: *"Though we want so badly to RUN through this hell, it's important to remember time with our kids is a construct that our kids are not necessarily going to adhere to. It's OK for milestones to come much later than expected. Keep* *celebrating progress even when it's in tiny steps with much backsliding in between achievements. Love them where they are, not where you wish they were."*

CJ: *"Be prepared for finding a counselor to be a process. This is difficult for everybody when they can barely function. Having to tell and retell their story to different professionals until they find the right fit can be overwhelming. I tried to encourage my daughter to give counselors too much time and grace. She has an eating disorder and many counselors are at a complete loss as to how to deal with it. We wasted way too much time finding a good therapist."*

EWM: *"This is a long journey but there is hope! Build your village. It's important to know that not all therapists are good therapists, and some can do more harm than good. Same with hospitals. Do some research, ask lots of questions, and follow your gut when it comes to your child's care. Get a therapist for yourself and join a support group. You will need other moms who truly understand. If you have a spouse, try to go to some therapy together so you can be on the same page and support one another. Make sure your child's school understands and embraces your child's condition. The school should be your ally, not your enemy. Request information on how you get a 504 for your child. If you feel the school administrators and counselors aren't educated in mental health, look for another school. And remember, tomorrow is another day. I used to get so panicked when my daughter refused to go to school. I have finally learned to give her space to try again the next day. The journey doesn't follow a straight line. Most of the time it is two steps forward and one step back. And that is OK! Most of all, let them know they have so much strength inside."*

CBD: "*Two big points I would make: First, don't compare your child or your decisions to those of neurotypical children. You will be judged harshly. Second, get help. Seek a counselor immediately because it could take a while to find one. Make sure you take the time to find one that matches your child and can offer you support as well. This can be a daunting task, but one that will be necessary for many years down the road.*"

LKH: "*I have learned from many wise mamas in my support group a number of things that I still struggle to implement:*

1. *Listen vs. Solve. I want to solve everything for her and that makes her feel like a burden.*

2. *Support vs. Enable. This is such a tricky one! One hundred percent support at all times, but that does not mean enabling, shrinking responsibilities, or covering for your child.*

3. *Empower vs. Solution. Provide options, alternatives, and caregivers, but let them engage in, and take ownership for, their own care and support system.*

4. *Trust vs. Worry. This is super, super hard. Moms will never not worry, but constant worry helps no one, us or them. We have to have faith that there are better days ahead.*

5. *Disengage vs. Provoke. So much of what I was doing to solve and fix was taking her and her situation head on and just amplifying her mood, distress, or anxiety. It feels so wrong, but disengaging is a better option.*

6. *Put your oxygen mask on first. It is so hard for a mom, but taking care of your physical and mental health so you*

can be strong for them is so important. If you are falling apart, how can you help?

7. *Let it go vs. Nitpick. There is so much that kids with mental illness are challenged to manage every day. Some things just aren't worth the fight. Think hair color, piercings, room condition (close the door), clothes . . . let it go!*

8. *Love vs. Instruct. I find myself giving so much direction and guidance that it is overwhelming for her. She just needs to know that I'm in her corner, I have her back, and I'm available when she needs help.*

9. *It takes a village. Get a support network. You cannot possibly be all things for your child. Get a professional, personal, social (if possible) network in place, and let your child rely on them.*

10. *Never give up! You are not alone. You are worth investing in. Your child is worth investing in. The world might not understand them, but you do and you are their best advocate.*

11. *Have fun! Lighten it up and just have down time. Make home/family a safe and fun place where all are supported and can have a good time. This sounds simple but can be extremely hard in practice.*

12. *Turn off the GUILT! It doesn't help or change anything. You make the best decisions you can in the moment and move on. You haven't solved this because it isn't solvable, not because you aren't hard enough, and you did not cause this."*

TTAW: *"Revel in the bright spots and commit them to your memory. When days, weeks, or months hurt, those simple joys* *will save you. For me, the simple fact that my fifteen-year-old with bipolar disorder, anxiety, and depression chooses to hold my hand on occasion is so simple, but such a gift. Find those things; the moments no matter how small can brighten your days."*

TMH: *"Over-caring and over-responsibility are trauma responses. They often come from a place of trying to control the uncontrollable. Give yourself permission to rest, let go of what is not yours to carry, and set boundaries."*

AB: *"Find professionals you can trust. If you are second-guessing the doctor or the therapist, you must find someone else. Also, you must be a savvy consumer of information. There is so much crap and bad information out there. You need to constantly check the science and sources of information behind recommendations. Trust your instincts."*
SA: *"Fight tooth and nail for every single aspect of treatment if you are being dismissed. Advocate, advocate, advocate. Do not be afraid to change psychiatrists or therapists, within reason, if there is a poor fit."*

KSL: *"Educate yourself and find support groups. The strength of my village of warrior moms has helped me through my darkest of days."*

RLG: *"Ask questions, give yourself grace, trust your instincts, and celebrate the milestones—no matter how big or how small."*

HHB: *"Find a therapist for yourself where you can process your experiences. A place where you can talk about the impact on you, without feeling guilty. My therapist is where I went* *to grieve my expectations for my kids, discuss my irrational guilt, and share what was happening with them to get another point of view. It's funny, now that both are so much better, my therapist celebrates their successes too. It's been invaluable. Also, practice self-care. I carved out my exercise time every day except when my son was hospitalized. I can't help them when I feel wound into a ball."*

KPK: *"We are often their safe spaces. This means we get to see the worst of them because we are the only place they feel safe enough to let it all out."*

FCR: *"What I've learned is: Go where the love is—it isn't always your family. My older sister told my seventeen-year-old daughter, driving her home from visiting her comatose twin sister, that we parents 'should have done more.' I've found such support from parents' groups, and my Al-Anon group. These people have learned not to judge, to listen, and to empathize. They validate that I am a good mom."*

CM: *"Mental illness in a loved one taught me to live in the present and treasure the person, not the illness."*

BP: *"Stay on the platform—don't board the ride when a loved one is going off the rails!"*

JM: *"Consider how hard it is to change yourself and you will see what little chance you have in trying to change others."*

CS: *"Here are a few things I have learned:*

1. *Never underestimate the power of going outside to stand in the rain together to calm a panic attack.*

2. *When the emotion and frustration of your teen is flowing out of them, validate their feelings. Validate again. There is no way to ignite the calmer, logical brain without this step.*

3. *The thought of taking a shower can be triggering for your teen if that has been a place of self-harm for them. On occasion, we put on a favorite, upbeat playlist and dance it out to a few songs* before sending her to the shower with the remaining songs in the playlist."

LK: *"A lesson my daughter—who is non-binary, dresses as pastel Goth, and has several unusual piercings—has taught me is to let all the preconceived ideas go. Even though we moms think we know what will be the simplest, easiest, and least hurtful road, it's still our kids' lives. They must make choices and live with them/learn from them. My kid knows I support them one hundred percent! That said, I give myself kudos when deserved too."*

ES: *"Middle school is when everything began to fall apart for my girl. Her coping mechanisms to cover her struggles could no longer keep up. She was diagnosed with depression, social anxiety, and ADHD. She is now graduating high school. We have had some good stretches and some really challenging stretches. Pandemic life has actually been a blessing in disguise. It gave her a break from the chaos in high school. High-volume crowded spaces are very draining on her. And like many kids who struggle as she does, she lost her friend group over the years. Shelter-in-place and remote school gave her a chance to slow down and not blame a lack of social interaction on herself. She's planning to go away to school in the fall. But, like everything in life, we'll deal with what comes along, all while doing my best to support and encourage her* *to be OK with setbacks, and to understand that life is a journey, not a race. It's corny sounding, but I think as long as she realizes she is loved even when she's feeling hopeless, there is always a glimmer of promise. We've had plenty of hopeless days and nights, but she is still here so that is a victory."*

CDN: "Some things I have learned:

1. *You'll struggle with your own friendships and family. Some will not understand your struggle, some will judge your struggle, and some will be your solid foundation. The third group are the relationships to hold dear and lean on.*

2. *Measure improvements or change not in days or weeks, measure in quarters of the year.*

3. *Your parenting skills will be challenged and need to grow. You will find it hard to relate to parenting challenges of your peers whose kids don't struggle with mental illness. But you'll gain a broader set of people skills that will make you a more compassionate human. I've gained way deeper friendships, partially because of the pain I've had to dig myself out of."*

Advice for Parents of Young Adults

The following section of advice comes from those whose kids are young adults. Much of this involves a less directive approach, because as our kids mature, they need to take increasing levels of personal responsibility for themselves. Effective parenting of children, teens, and young adults takes completely different skillsets, especially when mental health issues are present. We move from the role of a team manager to more of a sideline coach. Although we may be farther along on our journey of discovery, we may also have become burned out through our continued struggles with incredibly difficult day-to-day challenges. If we are lucky, we may have arrived at some degree of a new normal. We still seek to understand and utilize the best ways to survive and thrive with our beautiful and challenging KGs, regardless of their stage of life.

> *CCVV: "Something I have learned and I still struggle with is that your child's illness is theirs to manage, especially as they get older. As parents, especially moms, we want to handle it all. But someday they won't have us around and they need the skills to advocate and make decisions for themselves."*

> *SK: "Growing up in a strict religious family, I was raised to not talk about mental health. It was a shameful thing that we never discussed. I have since learned so much from raising two wonderful humans, both of whom have had struggles with anxiety and depression. I've learned that mental health is nothing to be ashamed of, and it is OK to seek help. I've learned who my real friends are. I am still working on talking less and listening more. As much as I would love to solve all of my kids' problems with a good lecture, that is not what they need from me. They usually need me to shut up and listen. I have also learned that wasting thousands of dollars buying my kids senseless things just to see them happy, even for just a few minutes, is by far my biggest downfall. I am still learning what works and what doesn't for each of my kids, as well as myself and my husband. Every day is different."*

> *LD: "Don't look back. You did the best you could at the time. No regrets. No beating yourself up."*

> *RE: "Don't lose your own interests. Raising a child with mental health struggles is a very scary, numbing path. Even if we have*

a professional background or training, nothing can prepare us for this terrible road. I got tons of bad information from professionals along the way. There came a point that I didn't trust my own ability to see smartly or clearly. Get a good therapist for yourself and open up to your most substantive friends. They can be a bastion of wisdom, even if they haven't been through mental illness."

BTP: *"Lead with love, no matter how hard. Always, ALWAYS let them know they are valued, loved, and that the world is a better place because they are here."*

NMS: *"Don't buy a ticket on their roller coaster ride! I've realized through the ups and downs it would affect me as well, both physically and mentally, when my daughter was struggling. I work really hard to remove my own emotions and just be there for support and validation as needed. I say out loud to myself, 'I am not getting on this ride today!'"*

DPG: *"The biggest lessons I have learned are:*

1. *People, even our children, have to want to take responsibility and try to feel better. I can lead them to the very best psychologists or psychiatrists, but ultimately they have to desire change and fight for their own growth. They have to feel like they are ready to do anything beneficial not to feel depressed or super anxious. It's the reverse of waving a white flag as a symbol of giving up. It's waving their hands by saying, 'I'll do it big, please stay by my side.' The lessons are knowing that we can't do this for them, they must want it more than we do for them.*

2. *Staying by their side is a parental lesson too. The days, weeks, months, and years can be tough, but very often*

we are all they have. They can be despondent or tough to be around, but we can't give up. As a byproduct of their disease, their friends often fall away. We become their entertainment or reason to get out of the house.

3. *Change and growth are not linear processes. Often, it is three steps forward, and two back. Eventually they move forward. Don't hit the panic button when they slide back a little. Even in normal life, no one changes and goes forward all the time. I hope this helps!"*

GGL: *"When my daughter hit her lows, I never left her side. I put a mattress down on her bedroom floor and slept there every night until things got better again. They are scared too, and just knowing someone is right there can bring so much comfort to them during the storm."*

CZ: *"I have learned that patience is key. It takes time to figure the path that works best. There is a lot of trial and error."*

JR: *"It truly is living through moments. Things can change from good to bad in a heartbeat. Cherish and hold on to good moments, and be ready for the bad. This is the most extreme roller coaster ride. Buckle up for the long ride and hold each other tightly."*

CSH: *"Join a group that gets it, truly. It's not bad parenting, shit just happens sometimes."*

DO: *"DBT!!! And boundaries! Both are so important. Also, know that your friends won't get it, and their lives will move on. You will create your new friends with those who do get it. And when it calms down you can, and should, reach back out to your other friends, because they probably miss you."*

NP: *"I have learned that grieving is necessary. This life is not one I ever imagined, and I need to show myself grace. I also dislike being told to go to therapy myself, because I did not want to rehash the bad. I needed to keep moving forward and be mindless. I still feel this need."*

RM: *"Choose relationship and connection. Drop the power struggles."*

CS: *"Spend less time asking yourself **why**, and more time asking **what now.**"*

MWO: *"Do not take your child's illness personally. I felt like a failure and I felt a ton of shame. Do your best, learn as much as you can, practice a ton of self care, and do as much of your own work as you can. We are not in control of the outcome, but we can play a positive role to the best of our ability."*

RLT: *"Always go with your gut. And hug the crap out of your child. Hold them tight and always love them and show them they are loved."*

BCB: *"Self care is not selfish. Learn all you can about the disease and treatment. Take family education classes. Learn DBT skills. You are not alone. Talk to your partner about your feelings—you don't need to be strong to protect him or her. And discuss trying to be on the same page or your relationship might not survive. Learn how not to enable and the difference between mental illness and being an asshole. And most important, trust your mama gut. If you think there is something wrong, there probably is. Push. Be That Mom. You might be the only advocate your child has, and if you don't do it no one else will."*

CS: *"Try not to waste mental energy on self-righteous friends and family who spew their simplistic explanations for your child's issues (participation trophies!). Then again, you'll need that mental energy to resist punching them!"*

BW: *"Know your truth. It's possible that your child's version of reality isn't what really happened. There are times when you may be portrayed as an abuser or villain. You need to know your truth to be able to get through it all, especially when you have specialists questioning your child's description of you. Also, don't overlook the needs of your other children. While my daughter was going through repeated hospitalizations, episodes of cutting, and suicide attempts, I specialized in 'triage parenting.' She got the lion's share of my time, and my other four boys all acted out. It's only now, twelve years later, that they verbalize how much they resented her and how much they needed me at that time. They get it now, as adults, but they shouldn't have had to."*

WRS: *"Don't forget that you matter, too. We do everything for our kids, and rightly so, but we are also humans and need love and care. Burnout is a very real thing. Pay attention to your own needs and take a break when the time is right. Rely on others to help out."*

LCR: *"I have learned to remember that I cannot change them into who I want them to be or have them take what I think would be a better path. I can only change the way I react. Otherwise, we go in circles, and nothing changes or gets better. I have learned to be an active listener, rather than one who waits to jump in with advice or a rebuttal. I have learned that for my son there are two non-negotiables for him to live under our roof: He takes his meds and he goes to counseling—even when he feels good. I have also learned that for me, working* *out and therapy are both a must. I get my dopamine levels up and my blood pressure goes down. And I get to evolve, grow, and learn more about myself through my own therapy instead of trying to have all the answers. Lastly, since I have children without mental illness and one with mental illness, it has become clear to me that sometimes their behaviors are selfish young adult actions rather than mental illness-related, so I would say don't get manipulated and jump to the conclusion that it is always mental illness-related."*

MSL: *"This isn't that positive, but the longer this goes on the more I realize that no doctor or therapist knows all the answers, and no treatment or medication is always right."*

KPK: *"I agree that they have to want to get better before they will make progress. I have lived on both sides of the equation with both of my girls.*

"It's not my fault, even though I dealt with my own depression before I had children. Our kids are their own people with their own health issues.

"Our kids are much more open about mental health than my peers and I ever were. My worries that their friends might find out about their mental illness were misplaced. It was more about my fear of my friends finding out. This fear led me to be careful about who to confide in. Some folks don't really care about you or your kid. But the ones who do care can care fiercely for you and your kids.

"Talk about strategies when you and your child are both calm. Ask them what they need from you when they are struggling. If they start losing it during this discussion, drop it. You can always come back to it. Going forward, utilize what you have learned from your conversations. Remember that it won't always work, but it will work some of the time.

"I know this isn't the case for all of us, but even though my husband was not always understanding, it turns out that he understood more than I gave him credit for. He just showed up in ways different from me. Because my girls always came to me first, his feelings were often hurt. And hurt people often hurt back—even when they are grown-ups. When push came to shove, he showed up in ways I couldn't.

"Let them know you love them always, but you don't have to always like them or their behavior. Not liking them doesn't negate your love."

HD: *"If you are walking on eggshells all the time, thinking 'I don't want to rock the boat,' the boat has already tipped and you need professional help.*

"Having an educational advocate, attorney, or educational consultant can make a big difference in outcomes and access to resources.

"The 'why' doesn't matter. Focus on how to move forward and let the therapists figure it out.

"You will probably get a new label every time you change doctors, and no one drops the old ones first.

"Ask yourself: If my child had diabetes, cancer, or a physical disease would I be this hesitant to use medications?

"Genesite was worth it despite what the doctor said. It was not perfect though.

"Unwell brains can't make good decisions. Sometimes I have to be the well brain, and make really hard ones.

"I didn't do this. It isn't my fault. I am doing the best I can to be part of the solution.

"The more I share our story authentically, the more I discover unexpected support from places I never imagined.

"There is an entirely new world of acronyms and other things I wish I didn't need to know.

"Mental health, especially in teens, is a lot of trial and error

"Residential treatment centers are not all the same

"Wilderness therapy is a thing—a crazy expensive thing, but worth investigating.

"I curse and cry a lot more, but it helps.

"Those who do judge are fearful it could happen to them if they can't blame me for what happened. Their fears are not my problem.

"There will be days when I love my child, but I won't like them.

"I am not alone and other families have survived this nightmare. There is hope."

PCR: *"Don't let your kids kill you. It is their journey. We can love but we can't fix. Chocolate is your friend."*

None of us voluntarily joined this KrazyClub, and it is not for the faint of heart! We learn and evolve through love and pain right alongside our KGs, and we also suffer some serious growing pains along the way. We must become smart consumers of medical care, learn the hard way to trust our instincts, come to understand and work better with boundaries, and practice staying open and loving, even in the midst of incomprehensible pain and confusion.

At the same time, there are many unexpected blessings along this difficult road, if we pay attention. Our hearts open, and we have the opportunity to become more compassionate, connected, and intuitive if we choose to. Our priorities shift in interesting ways, both large and small. We become wiser and more discerning about many things, including how and with whom we choose to spend our time. We learn these life lessons on the fly, under fire, without warning, preparation, or training. Then, we hone and refine our newfound skills, one crisis at a time. Warrior parents, I salute you. I humbly bow to your knowledge, wisdom and and grace. I am honored and privileged to walk with you, shoulder to shoulder, as we learn, heal, and teach alongside each other, together.

CHAPTER 10

Messages of Hope and Inspiration

"Deliver us serenity, deliver us peace.
Deliver us loving, we know we need it . . . "
—Kanye West

"Don't go blindly into the dark, in every one of us
shines the light of love . . . "
—Florence and the Machine

Hope is an elusive concept that means different things to different people. Some describe hope as an optimistic state of mind or a positive belief that something good or desired will happen. There are those who speak about hope strengthening their resolve and accompanying them through their hardest times, based on their faith, belief systems, or through the help of community support. According to Charles Snyder, psychologist and renowned hope researcher, "A rainbow is a prism that sends shards of multicolored light in various directions. It lifts our spirits and does not necessarily fade in the face of adversity; in fact, hope often endures despite poverty, war, and famine."

Mental illness presents unique challenges regarding hope. The insidious way that mental illnesses wrap themselves around our thoughts and feelings can make it hard to maintain a positive attitude or perspective. We need an optimistic mindset to remain committed to our goals and make the continued efforts necessary to move towards them. The determination to persevere through the inevitable challenges that come with creating a lifestyle of mental health and wellness are challenging. Therefore, we must work to cultivate hope, and when we hit a wall, be willing to find sources of strength and inspiration, to remain fortified to keep moving forward.

The emerging and powerful field called "positive psychology" is based on the belief and premise that people want to lead meaningful and fulfilling lives, while cultivating the best qualities within themselves. This school of psychology focuses on the strengths and positive potential of an individual, rather than on their weaknesses or pathology, to enhance their experiences of love, work, and play. There is also an area within the field of social work known as the strengths perspective. This approach puts the strengths and resources of people, communities, and their environments at the center of the helping process, rather than their problems. Both positive psychology and the strengths perspective highlight hope and mindset as important factors in positive outcomes for individuals and families.

There are many well-researched and documented benefits of having hope. Hope is correlated with superior academic and athletic performance, as well as greater physical and psychological well-being, improved self-esteem, and enhanced interpersonal relationships[17]. Individuals with higher levels of hope are more likely to view stressful situations as challenging rather than life-threatening, thereby reducing the intensity of the situation at hand.[18] Hope relating to chronic anxiety

---

17   Rand & Cheavens, 2012
18   Lazarus & Launier 1978

and panic disorder can be a protective measure, increasing confidence and reducing feelings of vulnerability and unpredictability [19]. Hope is also a motivational factor that can help initiate and maintain action towards self-care goals, thereby reducing signs and symptoms of depression[20]. These facts alone are hopeful, because like any other skill, a positive and forward-thinking mindset can be cultivated, and will expand and grow as it is practiced and reinforced.

In our darkest times, sometimes it can be hard to hold onto the hope that things will get better. We may question if we have the wherewithal to come through to the other side of our challenges. We may wonder how we will find the strength to continue. I remember my own hardest moments over the past years, where I was confused, heartbroken, angry, humiliated, despondent, or worn out. Many who live with mental illness will have times when we question if we are cut out for the task. We may feel completely overwhelmed or stretched thinner than humanly possible. During those times, the grace of others and their compassion, wisdom, and presence can go a long way in helping us to feel less alone and make it through to the other side of our despair.

The following messages are intended to act as balm to the weary soul and provide inspiration to carry on when the load seems too heavy to bear. We hope that all who need some words of strength and encouragement will find them here. Please let these heartfelt words assure you that that you are not alone, while helping you find the hope and inspiration to keep moving forward.

COURTNEY

Hope. This topic can seem strange and unattainable to those who are struggling, but keeping hope within ourselves is one of the best

---

19   Michael, 2000
20   Conti, 2000

things a KrazyGirl (or Guy) can do. There is always a bright light at the end of the tunnel, no matter how far we have to walk, or run, to find it. When we're having a tough day, it can seem like there is no end in sight. We might be exhausted, frustrated, or *hopeless*, but keeping a positive-ish attitude is crucial to actually feeling better. If we wallow in our pain and do not search for that bright light, we may not find it. If we stroll through the dark tunnel with an open mind and a gentle encouragement to "just keep swimming," we will find our way out.

This is a metaphor that I have kept with me throughout my life. I always work to remind myself that the tough days make the good ones that much more beautiful. I try to remind myself that if you look at the glass as being half empty, you will never see it as half full. You will never be able to acknowledge the good in life. When we are struggling with anxiety and depression, fighting through one tough day after the next, we tend to figure: *Well, I'm hurting so much right now, so what's the point of looking for the good in life? What's the point of waking up and giving life my all when everything I do backfires? My life never goes according to plan no matter how hard I try! I am hopeless!* Having this attitude will never bring us good. But I did not start to notice that until I introduced myself to mindfulness, gratitude, and acceptance.

Personally, my contemplative practices, such as doing yoga, meditating daily, keeping a gratitude journal, etc., help me look for the good in life, focus on loving myself, and loving life! I never thought I would wake up every day with excitement to take on life, but I did, indeed, get there. It was not by any means an easy process. It took retraining the neural pathways in my brain to help me to foster this positive outlook. Being hopeful, rather than hopeless, could be that one thing that changes your view on life. This pivot starts by changing our attitude from being a victim of our mental illness to taking power over our lives. We must gain control of ourselves and learn to look at difficult situations with a desire to be strong and push through the tough times, rather than giving in or giving up.

I *love* positive psychology. Learning about this method and using its themes and techniques in my own life has helped me adopt a positive attitude about life. I look at the strengths and potentials within myself rather than all my problems and struggles. I look to find the good in situations, rather than focusing on everything that can, or will, go wrong. I work to live a meaningful life and cultivate within myself everything that I aspire to be. I integrate things that make me feel good into every day. This may seem like nonsense or feel out of reach, but, I guarantee, taking bits of meaningful philosophies from this school of thought—or any positive field that brings joy—and working to integrate that into your everyday life is what matters most! After all, sometimes good things can only happen when we step out of our comfort zone.

My message of hope to you is this: Love yourself for who you are. Own your challenges and use them to help you become a stronger and more empathic individual. Look at difficult situations as a way to challenge yourself to become even more resilient. Find things to appreciate in life—not just technology or material desires. Channel the person you want to be and work to meet your goals. Work to make each day feel like an opportunity, rather than something that is going to be dreadful and drag on. Most importantly: Be kind to yourself, accept yourself for who you are, and work to make each day exactly what you want it to be!

Hope, From the Experts

Dr. Ed Barbarito, MD: *"There are always things that can help us. Find the right people to assist you along the way. And know things always work out, every bad thing has a good thing right behind it. You just have to look for it."*

Kelly Soloway, EYRT: *"No matter what you are going through, remember there are people in this world who love you. Also know that you are more powerful than you may realize."*

Donna Galarza: *"We are so fortunate to live in times where we know so much about the brain and the gut. It is now possible to get our brains and bodies as balanced as they can be, which can be life-changing in so many ways."*

Dr. Laura Richardson, PhD: *"There is so much evidence that DBT and trauma therapies work. There is hope. It works. There is family treatment. There are creative ways and resources available to afford therapy. Be persistent in getting the right treatment."*

Dr. Bruce Friedman, MD: *"No medication is perfect, but many can be useful tools on the path to feeling and being well. Always share details with your doctor, no matter how embarrassing they may seem. Anything a patient has shared with us is likely something we've heard a few times already!"*

Lani Bonifacic, LCSW: *"Help is absolutely possible but the whole family needs to be treated and, sometimes, not everyone is willing. If your loved one is suffering, please be willing to do the hard work of recovery yourself. Al Anon, CODA, professional therapy, are all available. Use them."*

Dr. Tina Sherry, PhD: *"There is a myth that people with eating disorders do not get better. With the right professionals and team, people can learn the right skills needed to recover. The earlier that treatment begins the better, so that ED behaviors do not get more ingrained."*

Lucy Pritzker, MS: *"If a family comes to me and I am able to give them hope, then I have been successful in helping them. Because if you don't have hope, you don't have anything."*

Rosalie Cespedes, LCSW: *"There is nothing permanent except change. We are creatures of evolution. We constantly change and evolve and that is OK!"*

Mary Cunningham, LPC: *"More and more teens are sharing their truth and experiences. It is not as shameful or embarrassing to be going through something now. In fact, it is pretty common to have struggles. I think that there is less judgement and stigma around seeking help and support in school today, and we are less alone and isolated when going through difficult times."*

Beryl Bender Birch: *"Just breathe. Call in your angels for help. Pay attention, because the answers you are seeking are there for you."*

Dr. Laura Berman, PhD: *"You are not alone. It may feel like there is no one else in the world that feels like you do, or it may seem like everyone else has it more together or is not struggling as much as you are, but that is not true. We are all struggling in some way and you are not alone. There is always help and you can become more empowered than you can imagine. Also, there are so many tools available, please avail yourself of them. Don't suffer in silence, don't suffer alone. Also keep in mind that what you resist, persists. If you allow yourself access to your authentic emotions, and maybe cry and allow some release, that emotion will pass in forty-five seconds to a couple of minutes. And then, you are lighter and clearer. Emotions are temporary and will pass, there is always relief and no mood lasts forever. This tolerance of your emotions will create resilience. Also remember, you may be the sanest one in the room, even if you feel Krazy sometimes!"*

Eric Kispert, LCSW: *"Hope comes from the inside. Hope comes from the outside. When I cannot recognize it within myself, I look to others to provide it. When the others around me cannot provide it and I cannot find hope in either place, it is a requisite that I must go to the Divine to seek hope and worth and value for myself during that period of hopelessness. The Divine will always prove hope if I seek it."*

Kalo Maloney, LICSW: *"Nothing ever stays the same, so that is hopeful right there. Change is inevitable—the bad times will pass because everything passes. You might be in pain right now, but you won't be in pain forever because it will pass. Hang in there."*

Hope, From Warrior Parents

One of the things that helped me the most and got me through some of my darkest hours when Courtney was struggling was joining a private Facebook group for (mostly) moms helping their teens and young adults through mental illness. I was a quiet lurker there for a while, then I started to give a little advice, then at some point I really opened up and bared my soul. This vulnerability was hard for me, due to the internal shame of being a helpful therapist to so many people, while at the same time feeling like a total failure as a mother. In this amazing space I found a diverse group of warrior moms from all over the world, who were also struggling on the same path. I recently reached out to this group, among a few of my other go-to groups (including the awesome KrazyGirls (& Guys) Survival group, of course) and asked if they could share some of their own messages of hope with us. I have so much respect and sincere gratitude for all of these fellow wellness warriors.

CWG: *'The dark days are oh so dark but remember, they make the brighter days even brighter. Always hang on to hope!"*

AM: *"This is all temporary. Breathe. Keep breathing."*

DO: *"Remember, you just don't have the skills yet. You would not expect yourself to drive a rocket ship without skill. Why are you expecting yourself to know it all without skills to deal with it? Seek out those who can teach you the skills."*

KE: *"Look for that thing that makes you happy and gives you peace. Whether it is music, art, writing, or sports, let it help you."*

BCP: *"What are you passionate about? What one or two things do you still love? Whether it is your dog, your drums, your poetry, your art, ice cream, reading, writing, or whatever else you love, use it as an anchor of hope. Your story isn't over. Keep holding on."*

AMC: *"There is always light in the darkness. Sometimes we need to sit in the darkness for a bit to find our true selves. Even on the darkest of nights, the stars shine bright."*

CC: *"You're never alone. You're stronger than you think. If you are in the dark, maybe you have been planted . . . soon you will sprout. Be patient."*

##: *"Nothing is wasted in life. Everything will enrich your body and soul. Please embrace yourself."*

LD: *"Reminder: You attract what you perceive and dwell upon. Shift your focus when necessary to another screen."*

ACD: *"My experience in the early part of my life was like a bouncing ball—putting out fires and bouncing from crisis to crisis. But I have learned to be intentional and now I direct that ball! I work very hard to be proactive instead of reactive to my mood and body states. Instead of reacting to situations, I now watch them, and I am proactive with my ball rather than my bouncing ball directing my life. I don't just let things happen anymore, I direct the course of my life, even with the very challenging things I must continually deal with."*

DD: *"Do not make permanent decisions based on temporary issues. And always come back to an attitude of gratitude. If you can feel grateful for what you have, you will be more able to be the captain of your own ship. Shift your focus to the positive and things will always go better. And that shift is always available to us."*

JW: *"I never appreciated the power of hope, until I had none."*

DPG: *"When we make a commitment to ourselves and honor it, we're building self-trust."*

BW: *"I was taught to meditate and practice grounding daily. Focus on being in the present moment. As you continue your practice, your view of the world will shift, and you will begin to see it differently. Pay attention to the messages you receive in meditation and seek to understand them, to understand the root of your problems and resolve them. Your relationship with the Source is not static. We are either moving towards it, or away from it, and that is up to us."*

TF: *"A moment of clarity fades like ash in the wind, yet a spark of hope keeps the faith. Something more on the horizon of lost thoughts flowing from the mind like a breeze, yet the world recycles and these things will arise again in a new light."*

DS: *"There is a place within all of us no matter what, which always remains whole and unbroken."*

LR: *"H.O.P.E.: Hold On Pain Ends."*

DA: *"Nature has a way of balancing everything out. In my hardest times, I always turn to nature."*

JMB:*" Do something each day for your future self. It may be something very small, like getting dressed, taking a walk, reading a chapter of a book. Tomorrow, your future self can look back on that accomplishment and build on it."*

AK: *"Music and dance can change inertia."*

SB: *"Just like in* Shawshank Redemption, *sometimes you gotta crawl through five hundred yards of shit to get where you need to be."*

KB: *"Choose you first. You are important and have value."*

MK: *"This will pass. Everything always passes. Hang on until the page you are suffering on turns."*

SJ: *"The greatest lessons I have learned were not during yoga or in a meditation class, but in the midst of my darkest moments. Ask the universe to help you see the lesson and move on."*

HS: *"Don't quit five seconds before the miracle! Try to forgive yourself and others. And most importantly, cultivate gratitude."*

TB: *"Prayer is powerful. I know that I got strength and support from the prayers of others who were praying for me during my hardest times."*

CCVV: *"When you are overwhelmed, try to focus on just doing the next right or best thing. Don't think about tomorrow or even the next hour. Ask yourself 'what's the next best step I can take right now?' For example, if the idea of finding a new treatment program is causing you anxiety, gather a notebook and pen, or open your laptop. Baby steps are still steps."*

JD: *"My favorite was given to me by a girlfriend. She said, 'Dealing with mental illness is like doing the cha-cha: two steps forward and two steps back, some dips and spins.' This thought gets me through the dark times, thinking of all the chaos as a dance."*

CK: *"I live by this quote from Anne Morrow Lindbergh: 'I want first of all—in fact as an end to these other desires—to be at peace with myself. I want a singleness of eye, a purity of intention, a central core to my life that will enable me to carry out these obligations and activities as well as I can. I want, in fact—to borrow from the language of the saints—to live in grace as much of the time as possible. I am not using this term in a strictly theological sense. By grace I mean an inner harmony, which can be translated into outward harmony.'"*

KG: *"Mark your calendar with colored dots that show what kind of day it was, and you may start to see a pattern that can give you reliable hope. For example, my child will put* *me through three weeks of hell and then may have a few good weeks. Then you can see how far away from that potential good week you are."*

CK: *"Natural habits encourage hope, like a good sense of humor, an optimistic outlook, and reminding myself, 'this too shall pass.' Take a deep breath and a break when needed. Chocolate doesn't hurt either."*

LG: *"Even though mental illness is a lifelong battle with its ups and downs, there is always hope. Things do get better and those on this journey grow up to be empathetic, compassionate, and strong. Trust them, mom, and trust yourself."*

DM: *"You can't outrun your problems. You need to meet them bravely, but the good news is that you're perfectly capable of that. Try something new, have patience, get right with God— whatever you need to do to make yourself strong enough is worth it."*

DF: *"Drive! Inspiration is fleeting because it is derived from the external. Drive must come from within. If you find out what you are passionate about and follow your passions, nothing will seem laborious again. The word 'work' doesn't apply to following your passions, it comes with ease."*

CK: *"It takes as much courage to have tried and failed as it does to have tried and succeeded."*

MKN: *"I've learned to reach out and let others know when I'm struggling. It can be really difficult to open up when you're shutting down, but people can't lean in to help if they don't know you need (and would welcome) support."*

KW: *"Trust your gut. Moms know their kids and need to trust their instincts. This shit is hard, but you are strong and you can be there for your kid. They need to know you are in their corner and will fight for them even when they cannot fight for themselves. Hang in there. Enjoy the good seconds, the good minutes, and the good days. Mourn what was, hope for what will be. It gets better."*

KG: *"There will always be some good days. And they will always be your child. Unconditional love is always there on both sides."*

JAB: *"I tell myself, 'I was selected to do this special job and to mother in such a special circumstance. I got this; I will stay strong and ride out this roller coaster yet again. Better days are coming.'"*

BLR: *"Trust in your own intuition when it comes to your child's care. NEVER give up. The hardest part is mourning the life you wanted for your child and accepting that is OK to let their path be different. Find others who understand your struggle, because sometimes friends and family won't get it. Do something for yourself to keep from getting sucked down in the quicksand with your child. And always hang on and have hope."*

DJ: *"I love this quote from Alexander Pope, 'Hope springs eternal in the human breast; man never is, but always to be blest. The soul, uneasy and confin'd from home, rests and expatiates in a life to come.'"*

MO: *"We all have our shortcomings, some more than others. Why I've been given this deck, I'll never know. But this I do* *know: Each day is a gift. Some gifts are wrapped all pretty, held together with a big bow. Some are wrapped in shit. Mental illness is not pretty. But somewhere, on some days, we find the gift and savor every single moment."*

CK:. *Sometimes in one's hectic life, we tend to hide and cover what we are truly feeling and going through. Sweeping it under the rug, covering with a bandaid, or putting the blinders on can be the easiest way to keep on an even keel. But then, life can spiral out of control. Recognizing is the beginning of recovery. The road to good mental health is steep when you begin and then, over time and with understanding and support, the path becomes a stroll."*

SIX LITTLE STORIES WITH LOTS OF MEANING

Author unknown

1. Once all the villagers decided to pray for rain. On the day of prayer all the people gathered but only one boy came with an umbrella. That is faith.

2. When you throw new babies in the air, they laugh because they know you will catch them. That is trust.

3. Every night we go to bed without any assurance of being alive the next morning, but still, we set alarms to wake up. That is hope.

4. We plan big things for tomorrow in spite of zero knowledge of the future. That is confidence.

5. We see the world suffering but still we get married and have children. That is love.

6. On an old man's shirt was written a sentence, "I am not eighty years old. I am Sweet Sixteen with sixty-four years of experience." That is attitude.

Epilogue

"And in the end, the love you take
is equal to the love you make . . . "
—The Beatles

Mental illness is a perilous road with an uncertain outcome. Having hope that things will improve can be challenging, and at times it can seem impossible.

It is my personal and professional experience that with the right treatment and support, mental illness *will* improve tremendously and stabilize for most people, most of the time. However, this is not always the case. It can be extremely difficult to navigate the complexities of the mental health system and for many, access or availability is a nightmare. Even with the best treatment and support, there are times when things do not get better, or even worse, end tragically. I know too many for whom this has been the case, and my heart breaks for their pain.

There have been many dark nights of the soul during Courtney's most challenging times when I feared that she, or I, would not make it. On this journey, I have felt the emotions and physical sensations of total exhaustion, hopelessness, rage, depletion, embitterment, embarrassment, terror, and deep loneliness among a million others. These emotions have waxed and waned throughout the years, and now are largely settled into our new normal, which is thankfully now, usually peaceful. The primary emotions I work to cultivate these days are gratitude and humility. Gratitude that I sleep with both eyes closed, no longer on the edge awaiting disaster to befall. Humility, because our lives could have easily unfolded differently. I truly believe that the grace of a loving force of benevolence walks with us, bringing the guidance and healing that led to Courtney's positive outcome. I have certainly prayed for this, at times on my knees, asking for the ability to *discern,* or be granted the wisdom to make good choices in the dark. I believe that all of our experiences, both painful and joyous, have propelled us toward our destiny— including writing this book, and starting the KrazyGirl Project. I know that this same force of grace will continue to guide us as we move forward on our path, and we will hurt, heal, learn and continue to teach as our lives unfold.

Like a wolf at the door, mental illness will always be a concern in our family, like many other families, requiring regular attention and awareness. However, as time passes, and I watch Courtney grow and thrive, I relax more and more. I no longer sit in on her appointments with her psychiatrist, and she determines the frequency of her therapy appointments. I usually trust her decisions and am starting to believe in her ability to know when she needs a course correction or medication tweak. I am extremely proud of her educational and professional aspirations and feel safe with her relationship choices.

Because of this, I, too, have moved forward with my life and am enjoying contentment as my new benchmark of happiness. As I wrote about in the Chapter on School, *"As young people begin to increasingly take on the lead role in the production of their own lives, parents will direct more from backstage and eventually we will come to sit in the audience. This natural process will ebb and flow as time passes on, and one day a new scene will set the stage for the next comedy or tragedy that is our life."* The wheel of life has now thankfully moved forward, and we are on our way with a sense of excitement for what the future holds. Like a child on the eve of a favorite holiday, I now have hope and faith that the new day will present with peace and joy.

It is our sincere desire that this book has been a helpful tool on your mental health journey, and that our experiences and the wisdom of the experts we interviewed paves a clearer path forward. KrazyLand is a dark and confusing place, and nobody should have to walk this road alone. As you travel, please have hope. Work hard for your wellness, help pave a path for your loved one, and hold their hope in your heart for them when they can't hold their own. Together, we look toward the future, where there is always hope in some form or fashion if we seek it.

XOXO Marci and Courtney

ACKNOWLEDGEMENTS

My deepest gratitude and appreciation for the many special people who have contributed to this guidebook. First and foremost, to my daughter and co-author Courtney Jessica Ober, who was the inspiration and reason this book and The KrazyGirl Project exists. Courtney, you are a kind, resilient, and passionate mental health advocate and I am so very proud of you. It is your destiny to do good things in this world. I also am deeply grateful to my amazing daughter Jordan, who struggled with our family through our darkest times, and emerged strong, compassionate, and dedicated to the wellness of our planet. I love you and I am proud of you, more than words can express. To my husband Henry, who gave me the space and time necessary to create this important work, I thank you.

To my lifelong best friend, confidante, and soul sister Jesse Brown; you have taught me the meaning of true friendship and unconditional love. I am forever better because of your presence in my life. Never leave me!

To my amazing colleagues that I am also blessed to call friends, I am so fortunate to keep your company! Eric Kispert, LCSW, you are an inspiring and brilliant mentor who helped me learn to be "relational" through my hardest life challenges. Kalo Maloney, LICSW, you are my lifelong trusted friend and fellow biker ole lady-turned-therapist, who knows me like no other. Dr. Bruce Friedman, there is no better psychiatrist out there—I deeply appreciate your brilliant mind and warm heart and will forever be grateful for your competent and compassionate care. Dr. Merijeanne Moore, I thank you for giving me my start in private practice and teaching me through example in my early days as a therapist in Alaska. Jamie Secol LCSW, there is no better practice associate, and I love practicing psychotherapy alongside you.

To badass editor, Landon Moores, this book would not be in the world without you! You expertly guided me through endless rewrites and structure corrections and patiently put up with my whining and sniveling. I am so glad we met in Cuba!

Publicist extraordinaire Gretchen Koss—you chose to become my agent because you believed in our work, and your tireless efforts and refinements contributed tremendously to our efforts. I appreciate you and your humor more than you will ever know.

Our KrazyGirl Project non-profit Board of Directors: Mike Ryan, Dr. Linda Nardone and Melissa Griegel—your tireless dedication and expertise allows us to achieve our goals. Gratzie!

To all the members of our diverse international Facebook community, I treasure you! Your meaningful and heartfelt participation through stories, sharing of experiences, and support of each other and mental wellness is the agent of change that makes a huge difference in the world. Keep on letting your love light shine! And to our group administrators and moderators including music director Bruve Van Hoven, humorist Kathy Shuey, thoughtful Susan Mazar and especially Niki Condurso, my podcast co-host, creative collaborator and soul sister, I cannot thank you enough.

The individuals, families and couples I have been fortunate enough to work with throughout my thirty years in practice—thank you for trusting in me and allowing me to work with you during your most challenging times. I sincerely hope our work together has been helpful. You inspire me, and I learn more from you than you will ever know.

For the amazing professional contributors to this book: Dr. Laura Berman Ph.D., Dr. Bruce Friedman MD, Dr. Danica Anderson Ph.D., Lauren Milner MA, Lucy Pritzker MA, Laura Richardson PsyD, Tina Sherry PsyD, Lani Bonifacic LCSW, Dr. Edward Barbarito MD, Donna Galarza, CN, Beryl Bender Birch RYT, Kelly Solloway RYT, Rosalee Cespedes LCSW, Ashley DiBiasi Ph.D., Mary Cunningham LCSW, Paul Barger Esq, Dr. David Nast Ph.D., Katharine (Kalo) Maloney LICSW, Eric Kispert, LCSW, Steven Donohue LSW, Sheila Newman MD—I am humbled by your knowledge and sincerely grateful for your generous, meaningful, and diverse contributions to this work.

To warrior parents and devoted loved ones who seek answers and provide support through meaningful participation in parent Facebook groups, I salute you. You define the word "hero."

For my fabulous publishing home Koehler Books, and our "Book Daddy" the incredibly unique John Koehler—thank you for taking a chance on us. Because of you and your wonderful staff, including Kellie, Kristin and Joe, our book is the best it can possibly be.

And to every human being who valiantly struggles with mental illness and carries on through dark times with hope for the light, this book is for you. May we all walk together, armed with the desire to move forward and to help others with our hard-earned knowledge, wisdom, strength and empathy. Our efforts will never be in vain.

About the Authors

 Marci Wolff Ober, LMFT, is a licensed Marriage and Family Therapist, mental health educator and advocate, with over thirty years of wide-ranging clinical experience. Professionally licensed in three states, Marci was a pioneer for MFT licensure in the state of Alaska and has served on the Executive Board of the New Jersey Association of Marriage and Family Therapists. Marci has had the pleasure of working with a wide variety of people in various states and settings, holding roles ranging from Therapist to Clinical Director of a major psychiatric hospital, and is also a certified yoga teacher. For the last twenty five years, Marci has concentrated her efforts on her private practice, Alternatives Family and Counseling Services in Northern New Jersey, and now works virtually with individuals, couples, and families all over the world.

Marci and Courtney are the co-founders of The KrazyGirl Project, a 501(c) 3 nonprofit organization, whose mission is to bust mental health stigma and promote wellness tools and education free of charge, for the benefit of humanity. Proceeds from *The KrazyGirl (& Guy) Parent Survival Guide* benefit our foundation.

Courtney Ober is a college student majoring in social work, working towards continuing her education as a Ph.D. candidate in clinical psychology. Courtney has earned her CDA (child development associate certificate), and founded a small business that provides teaching support and enrichment activities for elementary age children. Courtney's goal is to become a college professor, researcher, and to help others who suffer from mental illness.

Courtney has experienced the pain and confusion of dealing with mental health challenges at a young age, and has come out of KrazyLand stronger, wiser, and full of hope and compassion. Courtney shares her poignant story and unique perspective about what it takes to be mentally healthy and well as a teenager and young adult in our current age of artificial Insta-Perfection, where what you see is not always what you get. The truth Courtney shares is raw, vulnerable, uncut, and without any filters.

Please visit us at www.krazygirlproject.com

CPSIA information can be obtained
at www.ICGtesting.com
Printed in the USA
LVHW042302060322
712739LV00001B/62

Volatility views (*Continued*)
  and short straddles, 195,
    204–205
  and short strangles, 201,
    204–205
  and Vega, 191
  definition, 190
  monetization, 193,
    204–205
  volatility bearish, 190

  volatility bullish, 190
  volatility neutral, 190
Volatility, 72–80, 99–103

Zero-sum game attribute
  call option, 35–37
  definition, 15
  forward contract, 15–17
  put option, 57–58
Z-score, 83–84